British Armoured Car Operations in World War One

British Armoured Car Operations in World War One

British Armoured Car Operations 1914–1918

Bryan Perrett

Pen & Sword
AVIATION

First published in Great Britain in 2016 by
Pen & Sword Aviation
an imprint of
Pen & Sword Books Ltd
47 Church Street
Barnsley
South Yorkshire
S70 2AS

ISBN 978 1 47386 118 3

A CIP catalogue record for this book is available from the British
Library

Typeset in Ehrhardt by
Mac Style Ltd, Bridlington, East Yorkshire
Printed and bound in the UK by CPI Group (UK) Ltd,
Croydon, CRO 4YY

Pen & Sword Books Ltd incorporates the imprints of Pen & Sword
Archaeology, Atlas, Aviation, Battleground, Discovery, Family
History, History, Maritime, Military, Naval, Politics, Railways,
Select, Transport, True Crime, and Fiction, Frontline Books, Leo
Cooper, Praetorian Press, Seaforth Publishing and Wharncliffe.

For a complete list of Pen & Sword titles please contact
PEN & SWORD BOOKS LIMITED
47 Church Street, Barnsley, South Yorkshire, S70 2AS, England
E-mail: enquiries@pen-and-sword.co.uk
Website: www.pen-and-sword.co.uk

Contents

Maps

List of Plates

1. Plans of Mr Frederick Sims' 'War Car' that appeared in the April 1902 edition of *The Autocar*. The War Office was not impressed, commenting that 'However private gentlemen chose to spend their time was entirely their own business'. The car was vulnerable to any form of fire from above and the life expectancy of the commander's periscope could be measured in minutes.

2. Mr Sims, seen here manning a machine gun, was not, however, a man to give up easily. He managed to sell at least one of a smaller version of his car to an East African railway company which was tired of having its permanent way plundered by others who found alternative uses for the metal. These vehicles were fitted with flanged wheels permitting them to operate along the track.

3. When war broke out in 1914 it was the Royal Naval Air Service that convinced the Admiralty and, later, the War Office, that a use existed for armoured vehicles fitted with weapons. Many patriotic citizens, including a sizeable number of Rolls Royce owners, donated their vehicles for use in this way. The illustration shows an armoured Rolls Royce fitted with a machine-gun turret. Its Petty Officer crew are still wearing their blue temperate climate landing rig.

4. Active service revealed that the smaller cars sometimes required the assistance of a more heavily armed vehicle. These began entering service in 1915. Pictured here is a Seabrook heavy armoured car armed with a 3-pdr gun mounted on a turntable. If necessary, part of the side armour could be lowered, as shown. The gun could be dismounted for towing on a specially constructed carriage.

5. Another heavy armoured car which entered service in 1915 was the Pierce-Arrow, the 3-pdr gun of which was mounted in a traversing turret. On balance, the 'heavies' gave a good account of themselves, but their weight was a handicap in soft going. In theory, each armoured car section included one 'heavy'.

6. The RNACD section of Rolls Royce armoured cars committed to the fighting on the Gallipoli peninsula saw only limited action because the front resembled that on the Western Front, where movement was prevented by trench lines and barbed-wire entanglements. The cars spent most of their time in these dugouts, which offered some defence against the Turkish artillery, and took part in the general evacuation.

7. Hugh Grosvenor, 2nd Duke of Westminster, seen here in the uniform of the Royal Horse Guards (The Blues) raised an armoured car unit from among his friends and estate staff. The unit was despatched to Egypt when the Senussi invasion from neighbouring Libya threatened the political stability of the area,

8. A section of the Duke's units at one of its Egyptian bases. The young officer in the foreground together with his driver and fitter, are being photographed for 'the folks at home'.

9. The Duke's cars routing the Senussi at Agagyia, just one of the battles at which the unit earned its glamorous reputation. The artist was not familiar with Rolls Royce armoured cars, but his picture describes what happened accurately enough.

10. Once the threat posed by the Senussi had been dealt with, the Duke's unit returned to the UK and the security of the Western Desert became the responsibility of Light Car Patrols. These consisted of Model T Fords armed with Lewis guns, and motor cyclists. They produced the desert maps used in the Second World War and introduced many elements of desert safety including the priority of radiators for any water supply, air recognition panels, maintaining stated routes and adequate supplies of rations, vehicle spares and tyres.

11. Commander Oliver Locker Lampson MP RNVR commanded the most widely travelled armoured car unit of the First World War. Undoubtedly liked by his men, he employed unbelievably devious methods to obtain whatever he wanted but ruthlessly destroyed the career of an officer whose record threatened to outshine his own.

12. Part of Locker Lampson's unit, which consisted mainly of Lanchester armoured cars, attracting attention of local children as it passed through Trans-Caucasia on the first of its campaigns.

13. The Australian Armoured Car Section was an early arrival in Egypt. It consisted of (centre) a chain-driven Mercedes, which was later deprived of its turret; right, a Daimler mounting, first, a Renault 37mm cannon and, then, a Colt machine gun with gunshield, and (left) a Minerva tender. The section also possessed a motor-cycle combination armed with a Colt machine gun. The cars were returned to Australia in 1917. Some of the section transferred to the British 11th and 12th LAMBs (Light Armoured Motor Batteries), while others formed the 7th (Australian) Light Car Patrol.

14. The 7th (Australian) Light Car Patrol photographed shortly after its formation. The unit greatly distinguished itself, notably during the First Battle of Gaza.

15. A rare coloured photograph of No. 1 Squadron RNACD's Rolls Royce armoured cars at Kalkefeld in German South West Africa (present day Namibia) where it co-operated with South African troops.

16. Following the German surrender in South West Africa, most of No. 1 Squadron returned to the UK but four of its cars were shipped round the Cape and served in German East Africa, known then as Tanga and now as Tanzania. In this theatre the unit became known as No. 10 (RN) Armoured Motor Battery.

17. Campfire scene in East Africa. The Rolls Royce crew allow two *askaris* to examine what must have seemed a very strange machine indeed.

18. Also serving in East Africa was an armoured car unit raised privately by Sir John Willoughby, a participant in the Jameson Raid. Sir John insisted that his four-car battery should be known as No. 1 (Willoughby's) Armoured Motor Battery – the crew's neck protector cloths, not seen since the Battle of Omdurman, provide a nice 'private army' touch. The Leylands were well designed in many ways but were too heavy for what was asked of them in East Africa, witness the deep rutting caused by the wheels despite their being fitted with wide flanges.

19. The 4.1-in guns salvaged from the German cruiser SMS *Konigsberg*, sunk in the Rufifi river by the monitors HMS *Severn* and *Mersey*, would have provided the British armoured car crews with a headache had they been employed against them.

20. The Government of India was responsible for the conduct of the war in Mesopotamia. It despatched two Fiat armoured cars to General Townshend, who was conducting an ill-conceived advance on Baghdad. One is seen here being unloaded from a barge on the Euphrates. Both cars fought at the Battle of Ctesiphon, which resulted in a British victory although the heavy casualties sustained forced Townshend to withdraw.

21. Both cars survived the retreat and were not involved in Townshend's disastrous surrender at Kut-al-Amara. Fitted with flanged wheels they were used to patrol the railway line that brought supplies from Basra to the Front and eventually reached Baghdad when the Turkish front was broken. The car in the illustration has been fitted with extra shade against the sun and has two chuggles (canvas bags fill with water) slung behind the cab. Evaporation kept the water cool.

22. When the Turkish army's front was broken in 1917 its retreat quickly became a rout. The scene was sketched as it developed by Private Bagot of the 14th Hussars. On the left the gunboats *Tarantula*, *Mantis* and *Moth* are pursuing a Turkish gunboat; in the middle distance the guns of S Battery RHA are in action and a

30. Another of Dunsterville's problems was supply. It had taken this convoy of Model T Fords a week to cover the road from the unit's main base at Baghdad to Enzeli, crossing mountain ranges like that in the background while the summits of other passes were covered in snow and the blistering heat of the plains was replaced by freezing high altitude cold.

31. A local warlord named Mirza Kuchik Khan also tried to get in Dunsterville's way but was finally persuaded to return to civil life by a charge of kukri-wielding Gurkhas led by an Austin armoured car that dispersed his followers. He promised to be good and was allowed to keep his expensive automatic for his own defence.

32. Another poor but interesting photograph showing one of Duncars' Austins in an area of the Baku oilfields known as The Mud Volcano, where some of the heaviest fighting took place.

33. Lieutenant Colonel E. J. Carter, commanding the 17th Battalion Tank Corps, beside one of the battalion's Austin armoured cars, which were armed with Hotchkiss machine guns. The upper part of the vehicle is painted sky blue to aid concealment on crests.

34. To counter unrest in various parts of the sub-continent, often fomented by German sympathisers, the Indian Government produced a hybrid armoured car/personnel carrier, simply known as the Indian Pattern armoured car. This prototype, patriotically named *The King-Emperor*, is providing senior officers with a sample ride.

35. The Indian Pattern armoured cars were constructed by railway workshops throughout the country. The builders stuck to the basic plan but introduced local variations in design. Some were fitted with a frontal girder like a submarine's net cutter; this was intended to cut cables or ropes that had been stretched across the road to decapitate crewmen.

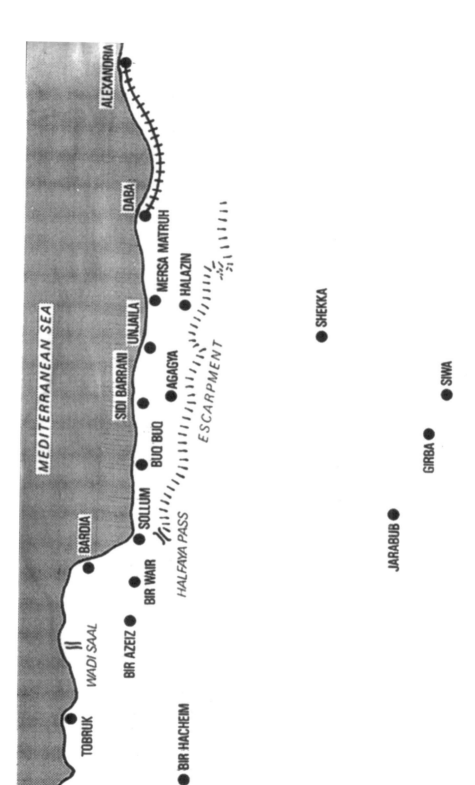

Map 1. The Senussi War.

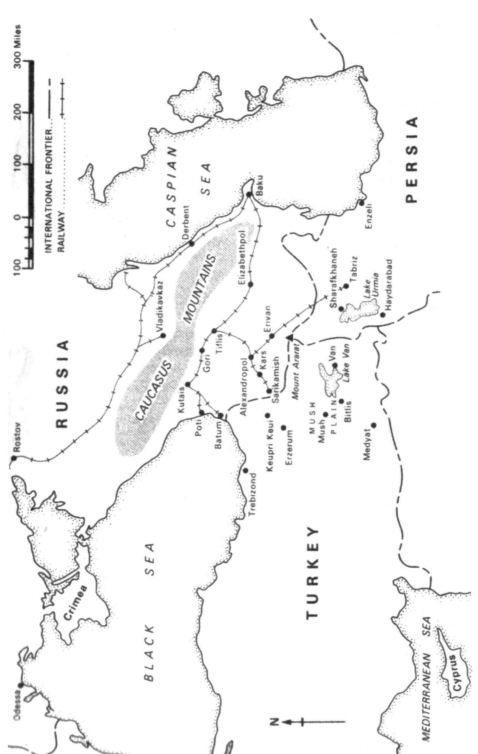

Map 2. Operations in Trans-Caucasia.

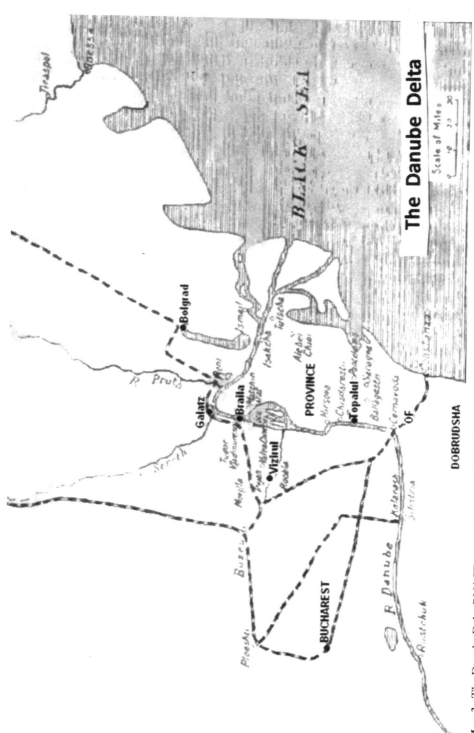

Map 3. The Danube Delta RNACD operations against Bulgarian troops in the Dobruja area of Romania.

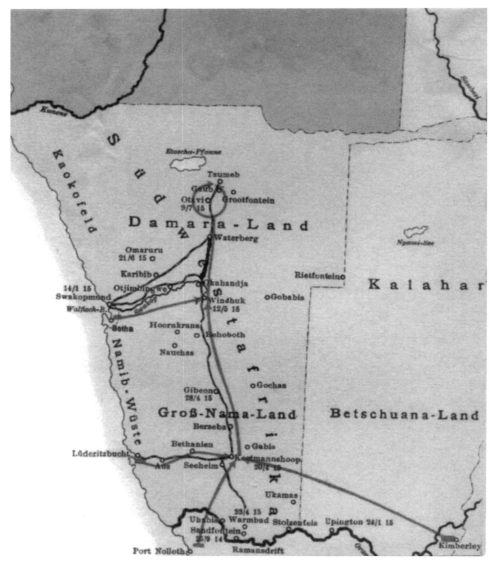

Map 4. A German map of South West Africa, showing the concentric invasion routes of British and South African columns, 1914–1915.

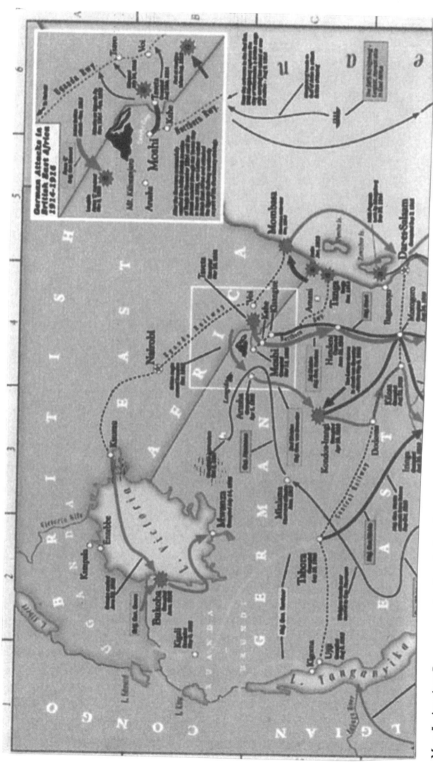

Map 5. Another German map showing the frontier area between the German colony of Tanga and British East Africa 1914–1916.

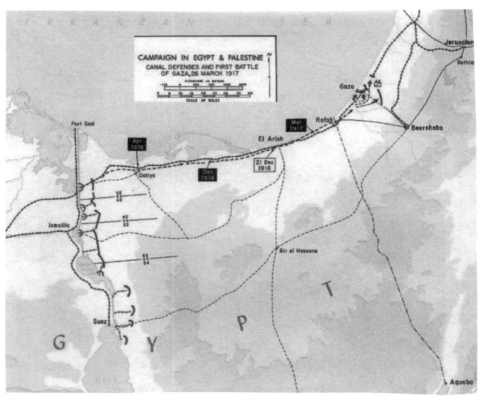

Map 6. The Campaign in Egypt and Palestine.

Map 7. Operations in Mesopotamia.

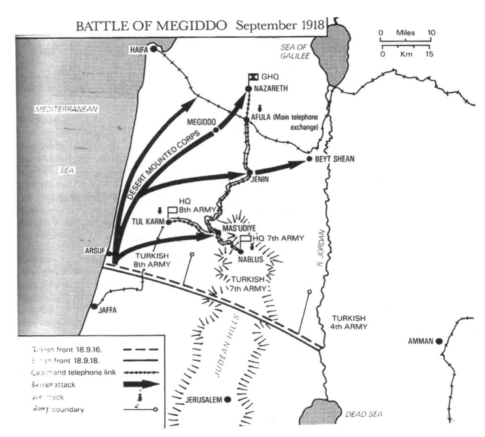

Map 8. The Battle of Megiddo.

Foreword

Prior to the outbreak of what became known as the Great War, very few professional armies were interested in developing the armoured car as a weapon system. The three traditional arms, infantry, cavalry and artillery, could not see a use for them in their own operational sphere, although it was suggested that in Imperial Russia the police might find them a useful tool when it came to putting down the riots of the downtrodden masses. Over the years, various inventors had struggled to push the idea of a self-propelled vehicle armed with an automatic weapon in a practical form. Some were downright dangerous to everyone in sight, but a few showed promise. In the United Kingdom, the first months of the war produced a recognition that there were uses to which a vehicle combining the elements of movement, protection and firepower could be put. Indeed, many of the first units to be formed were equipped with private cars donated by their owners, suitably armoured and armed in accordance with their probable use.

At first, it was the Royal Navy that manned the cars; then they were transferred to the Army's Machine Gun Corps; and finally they became the responsibility of the Tank Corps, which added the prefix Royal to its title in 1923 and finally became the Royal Tank Regiment. The Great War saw British armoured car units serving in Belgium, France, Egypt, Libya, Gallipoli, the German colonies of South West Africa and East Africa (now known respectively as Namibia and Tanzania), Russia, Romania, Mesopotamia (modern Iraq), Arabia, Palestine (now Israel and Lebanon), Syria, and Persia (Iran).

The most travelled unit of all belonged to the Royal Navy and was commanded by a somewhat tricky Member of Parliament named

Oliver Locker Lampson. It spent much of its time in Russia, where it fought Turks in Trans-Caucasia, Bulgarians in Romania and Germans and Austrians in Galicia. After the Revolution it managed, narrowly, to avoid an armed confrontation with the Bolsheviks and was withdrawn to the United Kingdom. There it passed to Army control and was re-equipped before being transported to Mesopotamia. It then made an epic drive across Persia, fighting a successful battle or two with a local warlord before reaching the port of Enzeli, from which part of the unit was shipped across the Caspian to Baku in southern Russia where it assisted in the defence of the local oilfields against a major Turkish advance long enough to prevent any of its priceless oil reaching Germany or Austria-Hungary before their surrender in 1918.

Tony Lord and I had both spent a considerable time researching the history of the unit and decided to pool our resources some thirty years ago. The result was a book entitled *The Czar's British Squadron* which was published in 1981 by William Kimber. It was well received and sold its entire print run. Shortly after, Kimber ceased trading, although demand for the book remained high and, before Tony passed away, he was able to see its price in the second-hand market reach levels beyond the reach of the average purchaser. Today, the price quoted for a copy showing obvious signs of use is £49.99, while a copy in mint condition sells at £171.40.

There are a number of practical difficulties inhibiting the reprinting of the book, the most obvious being that the amount of water that has flowed under the bridge since its initial publication has brought with it items of information that, while interesting in themselves, would neither alter the facts as stated nor justify the expense of insertion. Again, the object of the present volume is to tell the story of British armoured car units as a whole during the Great War. For obvious reasons, notably the extensive experience of the unit mentioned above, I have included several revised chapters on its history. However, there are remarkable incidents in the history of all the units I have mentioned. In the days of Empire and what has become known at

Global Outreach, servicemen could suddenly find themselves serving in unexpected areas of the world. This was seldom questioned and its acceptance was reflected in the words of a soldiers' song of the time, sung to the tune of 'Auld Lang Syne':

> *We're here because we're here,*
> *Because we're here, because*

and so on for several more identical verses. They were there, of course, because they had a job to do and, as I hope this book shows, they did it.

Bryan Perrett
February 2015

Chapter 1

Not Our Sort Of Thing At All, Old Chap

Today, it is quite possible that not one person in ten thousand has heard of Francisco Guicciardini, but for the record he lived during the Renaissance and wrote a book entitled *The History of Italy* in which he included numerous perceptive – and probably actionable – pen portraits of the most important personages of this time. One such portrait was of Ludovico Sforza, who rose to become Duke of Milan following the mysterious death of his nephew. Sforza, Francisco commented, had many excellent qualities, but was also vain,

his mind full of ambitious, restless thoughts ... and he violated his promises and pledges, always presuming so much on the basis of his own knowledge that being highly offended whenever the prudence and counsels of others were praised, he convinced himself that he could turn everyone's ideas in whatever direction he pleased by means of his own industry and manipulations.

During this period it was fashionable for such men as Sforza to patronise artists and men with interesting ideas. One of his beneficiaries was the genius Leonardo da Vinci, whom the duke brought to Milan. There, Leonardo painted a portrait of the duke's mistress, designed a huge equestrian statue of the duke's father, and undertook all sorts of engineering work. He was one of the world's great doodlers and his notebooks are full of all sorts of mechanical ideas. One of them pleased him so much that in 1492 he hurriedly penned the following note to his patron, who was also concerned with military matters:

I know how to construct secure and covered wagons for the transport of guns into the enemy's lines and not to be impeded by ever so dense a mass and behind which the infantry can follow without danger.

He enclosed a sketch of his invention which showed a circular vehicle protected by an umbrella-shaped canopy covered by iron plates. In the hull below, eight men turned cranks connected to the gearing that turned the axles of the vehicle's four wheels. Between the canopy and the hull were a number of gaps through which firearms projected. What he had produced was a combination of firepower, protection and movement, the essential elements of any fighting vehicle design and, five hundred years later, it became the accepted truth that Leonardo had designed the first tank. He hadn't, of course, but he can be credited with designing what was recognisably the first armoured car. However, in his enthusiasm to attract the duke's interest, he made a number of serious mistakes. No means of steering the vehicle had been provided, so that it could, in theory, only move forwards and backwards. In fact, it couldn't do either, because when the cranks were turned the gearing revolved the front and back wheels in opposite directions, a fact verified when, in recent years, the Tank Museum at Bovington built a model following the precise details of Leonardo's drawings. This was capable of correction but, if Guicciardini's opinion of the Duke was accurate, the latter would have spotted the flaws at once and declined to contribute funds for its construction. Had it been built, two further flaws would have revealed themselves. First the low power-to-weight ratio would have kept its speed down to a crawl and failed to cope with anything but the gentlest slope. Second, the heavy ground pressure would have seen it bog down in even moderately soft going. And that was that, for a very long time to come.

It was not until the nineteenth century that the steam railway revived interest in the possibility of producing a wheeled armoured fighting vehicle. Armoured trains consisted of a locomotive encased in armour plate and several open-topped trucks similarly armoured and mounting guns and/or automatic weapons as well as being loop-holed so that the infantrymen aboard could use their rifles. The function of such trains was to guard stretches of the line that were simultaneously of strategic importance and vulnerable to enemy activity. The influence of such trains was restricted not only by the track on which they travelled but also by the range of the weapons they mounted. Perhaps the most cost-effective armoured train in British military history was that employed by the garrison of Mafeking, which constructed a spur off the main line to bring a sensitive area of perimeter defences within range.

Nevertheless, the true armoured car had to await the appearance of the internal combustion engine before it could demonstrate its flexibility, and even then there were several false starts. Of these the best remembered was the so called Motor Scout. This consisted of a single-seater quadricycle powered by a 1.5hp engine and armed with an air-cooled Maxim machine gun for which protection was provided by a small bullet-proof shield. A photograph exists of its designer, Mr Frederick Simms, demonstrating the vehicle at Richmond in June 1899. His well-brushed bowler hat, shiny shoes and smart suit give the impression of an amiable eccentric, but the fact was that Mr Simms was a well-respected automotive engineer who had been commissioned to produce the Motor Scout the previous year by Vickers, Sons and Maxim Ltd in the belief that they had spotted a gap in the market.

Naturally, there were no takers for such a flimsy contraption, but Mr Simms' appetite had been whetted and he had already designed a boat-shaped motor rail-car with flanged wheels for the East African Railway Company. The problem was that the local people liked the new railway so much that they regularly dismantled bits of it to take home and put them to other uses, so that stern measures were needed to dissuade them. The rail-car was driven by a 7hp Panhard engine capable of producing a speed of 30mph in both directions. The hull descended to the level of the rails, ensuring that obstacles placed on the track were pushed aside without causing damage. Armament consisted of a 1-pounder Pom-Pom and a Maxim air-cooled machine gun and a searchlight was fitted for night operation. The vehicle was built in 1899 and shipped to Nairobi before being transferred to South African railways for employment during the Boer War, but its ultimate fate remains unknown.

In 1902 Simms produced the first British armoured car in conjunction with Vickers, Sons and Maxim. Known as the Simms War Car, it absorbed lessons learned during the Boer War. It was boat-shaped with sharply-pointed bow and stern, was twenty-eight-feet long, ten feet high and eight feet wide. Power was provided by a Simms-Daimler 16hp engine capable of producing a maximum speed of 9mph. The vehicle was open topped with the driver seated centrally, his only source of vision being two unprotected mirrors arranged periscopically. Simms provided for a Maxim machine-gun turret at each end of the vehicle, but these were not fitted when the car was demonstrated at the Crystal Palace in April 1902. Instead, two water-cooled Maxims were mounted at the front and a 1-pounder Pom-Pom at the rear. Judging by the number of top hats visible in and around the car in a photograph of the event, Simms had invited the entire British Establishment and everyone had turned up except, pointedly, any representative of the War Office. The attitude of this body was summed up in its own cold comment: 'Whatever private gentlemen choose to do in their spare time is none of our business.' This attitude was mirrored in almost every war ministry throughout Europe. The senior figures in these establishments were, in the main, elderly generals who had grown up in an era when wars were fought by marching infantry, mounted cavalry and horse-drawn artillery, and while those who had fought in South Africa absorbed the lessons of concealment and movement coupled with aimed rapid rifle fire, they could still argue that the war had been won by these three arms, even if it had taken far longer than had been expected. Why, then, should anyone want to introduce such new-fangled devices as armoured cars about which no one knew anything, thereby creating a new, unwanted and (apparently) unnecessary dimension to the battlefield. The infantry were satisfied with their improved musketry and machine guns and, for the moment, lacked the necessary technical support to maintain such vehicles in the field; the cavalry poured scorn on the idea that their work could be carried out by machines manned by rude mechanicals; and the artillery saw no role for them in its traditional methods of fighting. 'Not our sort of thing at all, old chap,' was indeed the verdict of many generals discussing the idea in their clubs.

Yet the 'private gentlemen' so scorned by the War Office persisted in their enthusiasms. It was clear that the younger generation of officers saw the benefits of combining mobility with firepower. In the Regular Army they could only follow the established doctrines and await events, but in the part-time Territorial Force officers were prepared to put their hands in their pockets to produce what they believed to be the right answer. The contemporary scrapbooks of many Territorial infantry battalions frequently contain photographs of one of the officers' tourers modified to tow a medium machine gun on a specially designed mounting.

Nor was interest on the continent entirely lacking. In 1904 the Austro-Daimler organisation produced its *Panzerwagen*. For its day, this was a very advanced vehicle indeed, being capable of a top speed of 28mph with an operational radius of 155 miles on full fuel tanks. It also possessed four-wheel drive, giving it a good hill-climbing and cross-country performance. The domed turret provided ports for one, increased to two, water-cooled Maxim machine guns. In 1905 the car was demonstrated at the Imperial German Army manoeuvres, followed in 1906 by a second demonstration at the Austro-Hungarian Army manoeuvres. For the reasons mentioned above, neither expressed anything more than polite interest.

Germany did, however, build two specialist armoured vehicles. During the Franco-German War of 1870-71, Paris was besieged and its garrison sent out official communications, plus microfilmed private letters for which a modest charge was paid, by means of hot air balloons. These were chased by German cavalry patrols and fired at by the German field artillery with very limited success, much to the enjoyment of Frenchmen who had little else to be pleased about. Not to be caught wanting again, the German Army developed two *Ballon Abwehr Kanone*, the *Panzerkraftwagen Ehrhardt* 50mm BAK in 1906, and the much improved Flak auf Daimler *Panzerkraftwagen* 57mm BAK in 1909, which incorporated a traversable gun mounting. These high-angle weapon systems were designed to engage the enemy's scouting aircraft and dirigible airships and also, if the range permitted, his tethered observation balloons.

The first army to take armoured cars into action was that of Italy. By 1912 it was clear that the extensive Ottoman Empire was in such a ramshackle state that its disintegration was imminent. Italy wished to expand her colonial holdings in Africa and had set her eyes on the Turkish province of Libya. Picking a fight was a simple matter and the Turks' inability to defend their overseas territories adequately ensured their ultimate defeat and surrender of the province to Italy. In technical terms, the Turks were outclassed from the start, for the Italians committed airships, aircraft and armoured cars to the fighting. The armoured cars included several Isotta-Fraschinis, which had been built the previous year. The car's manufacturers were an internationally famous motor-racing stable and despite its 3-ton weight the engine could produce a top speed of 37mph. Solid rubber tyres were employed and the front wheels were fitted with steel flanges to assist movement on soft going. In 1912 the Isotta-Fraschinis were joined in Libya by the first Fiat armoured cars. Fighting was confined to the coastal areas as the Italians had little interest in the vast, almost empty desert areas of the interior where so much fighting would take place thirty years later. Consequently, the cars' primary functions were as mobile machine-gun posts, providing fire bases for offensive operations and performing escort duties. Two at least were still active in 1941 but by then were clearly beyond first-line usage and had probably been relegated to police duties.

In 1902 the French company of Charron, Girardot and Voigt produced a semi-armoured car that attracted interest but no purchasers, probably because of dangerous vulnerabilities. Encouraged, the company produced two fully armoured vehicles in 1904. While unattractive to the eye – they resembled an armoured delivery van – they followed the layout that would be used by armoured car designers for nearly two generations, namely a front-mounted engine and a fully-enclosed hull mounting a traversable turret housing a machine gun. One interesting feature of the Charron cars was their self-sealing tyres. Of the two that were built, one was bought by the French Army and sent to Morocco to overawe a restless population and the second was purchased by the Imperial Russian government. This was not for the Army, who remained disinterested in the subject for the moment, but predictably for the police, who were having to deal with serious rioting in St Petersburg during the 1905 Revolution. It proved to be so much more effective than any number of whip-wielding Cossacks that the government ordered another ten from Charron, which became a British company in 1906. Only nine of these had been delivered by the time war broke out in 1914. Two had been confiscated by German customs officials while in transit to the customer and trialled in the Imperial Army's 1909 manoeuvres and it is possible that only one was returned to its rightful owners.

On the eve of war in 1914 the Russian Army's General Staff changed its mind about armoured cars and submitted the first of many orders to the Austin Motor Company Ltd for its twin-turreted car. This was based on the chassis of Austin's own 30hp 'Colonial' car which had a maximum speed of 45mph. Austin despatched a large number of these chassis to the Putilov Works in St Petersburg for completion. Cars completed in Britain were also despatched to Putilov for fitting with thicker Russian armour and staggering the position of the formerly side-by-side turrets to provide a wider field of fire for their machine guns. The Russian work seems to have been carried out badly, leaving gaps between the armour plates through which the enemy's fire could and did penetrate. The British-completed chassis included duplicate rear steering, enabling the crew to reverse out of trouble if the need arose. Pneumatic tyres were fitted for road use, replaced by studded rubber tyres for cross-country work. Russia also imported armoured cars from many sources, including another twin-turreted vehicle, the futuristic Mgebrow-Renault, so that by the end of 1916 she could field almost 200; but that is another story.

Chapter 2

Jack Tar Takes a Hand

The outbreak of war in the late summer of 1914 was greeted by cheering crowds in the capital of every belligerent nation in Europe. Since 1871 the continent had enjoyed a long spell of uninterrupted peace and war was an unknown experience to most people, who little understood that in the intervening years weapons had been developed that would inflict death, injury and destruction on an industrial scale. During the next four years empires would vanish, thrones would fall and the world would change forever. In their millions the reservists of the continent's huge conscript armies headed for their depots while in the United Kingdom, which maintained a small regular, but efficient and experienced, armed service, men in their hundreds headed for the recruiting offices in the hope of being in time to take part in the Great Adventure, which was not expected to last beyond Christmas.

A British Expeditionary Force, consisting at this stage of two corps and a cavalry division, was transported across the Channel to France with speed and efficiency, followed by the aircraft of the Army's Royal Flying Corps and the Royal Naval Air Service. The latter had been formed in 1912 with the principal task of scouting for the fleet. At the end of August 1914 its Eastchurch Squadron under Commander R. C. Samson established a base near Dunkirk having previously landed at Ostend to support the Royal Marine Brigade, which was for the moment attached to the Belgian Army. From the very beginning of the war the Belgians had been using private Minerva and Excelsior touring cars to shadow the German advance. At first, officers had used sporting rifles to bring down an enemy lancer or two, but it was soon realised that far more damage could be inflicted if Maxim machine guns were mounted on the cars. Several raids were carried out but in one of these the popular Prince de Ligne was killed. As a direct consequence of this, armour plate was fitted to the cars and, by the end of the first week in August, the conversion of tourers into armoured cars took place at Antwerp.

Samson lacked aircraft for his reconnaissance missions and decided that these could be supplemented with commandeered cars, which were also armed and could be used to rescue pilots who had been forced down between the lines. These adventures came to the ears of Winston Churchill, who was then serving as First Lord of the Admiralty. They appealed to his own piratical instincts and, in October, he decided to form a wing of the RNAS to become known as the Royal Naval Armoured Car Division under the command of Commodore Murray Sueter. The RNACD had its headquarters at 48 Dover Street, off Piccadilly, and a depot at Wormwood Scrubs under Lieutenant Commander Boothby. Suitable vehicles, of which the majority were Rolls Royces and Lanchesters, were either commandeered or made available by their owners. They were given strengthened axles and stripped of their coachwork, after which they were fitted with solid tyres, armoured bodies and a turret with all-round traverse mounting a machine gun. As originally planned, each RNACD squadron would consist of twelve armoured cars, sub-divided into four sections each of three cars. It was, however, anticipated that the enemy would develop his own armoured cars and that a machine-gun duel between opposing cars was unlikely to produce a result, armour-piercing ammunition having yet to be developed. The decision was therefore taken to develop a Heavy class of armoured car based on the chassis of a Seabrook or Pierce-Arrow lorry, mounting a 3-pounder gun that could not only knock out enemy vehicles but also destroy machine-gun posts and field artillery positions with direct fire. In theory, each section had the support of one Heavy, but in some units the Heavies were grouped together in their own squadron for ease of maintenance.

Naturally, a large number of drivers, fitters, and vehicle electricians would be required and in this respect the RNACD immediately found itself in competition with the Army, in which the Service Corps was expanding its mechanised branch. The problem was that this was a seller's market, for the fact was that motoring was in its infancy and very few men could drive, let alone maintain, a motor vehicle. Those who could were either well-to-do individuals with private means, professional chauffeurs, commercial vehicle drivers or members of the embryonic motor manufacturing industry. There was a keen competition for their services which the Navy was determined to win. On its behalf the Automobile Association set up examining boards in the leading hotels of the major cities. The successful candidates were rewarded with the minimum rank of Petty Officer Mechanic with the appropriate rate of pay, which far exceeded the Army's offer of a private soldier's uniform and remuneration.

Volunteers came from all over the United Kingdom, from all the Dominions and the entire Empire. The concept of the RNACD caught the public imagination and the Admiralty had no hesitation in accepting offers from wealthy individuals and groups to pay the cost of raising, equipping and manning its squadrons. The most notable of these benefactors was the Duke of Westminster, believed to be the richest man in the kingdom, who raised No. 2 Squadron from among his friends, neighbours and their employees, being rewarded with its command. The squadron was equipped with Rolls Royces.

On the British sector of the Western Front, cars continued to carry out most of the scouting missions. On 4 September Samson was personally carrying out such a reconnaissance mission when he ran into a car containing a party of German officers on the Cassel-Bailleul road. Samson's Maxim opened fire on the enemy car at 500 yards range, wounding two of its occupants, after which it hastily vanished in the direction of Bailleul. Next day, four British cars, three of them armed, approached the outskirts of Lille. An accompanying aircraft, piloted by Lieutenant Dalrymple-Clarke, had instructions to fire a Very light if the enemy were sighted. They were not and, entering the city, the cars were able to report the fact. This operation, while minor in itself, marked the beginning of co-operation between aircraft and armoured cars. Samson subsequently commented that a reasonable force of armoured cars, supported by aircraft, could have caused serious disruption to the German advance across Belgium and into France. This was not altogether wishful thinking, for Brigadier General Baker-Carr, who began the war as a gentleman chauffeur and ended it commanding a brigade of tanks, commented of this period that he had passed unmolested through the German lines.

However, the mobile phase of the war on the Western Front ended very quickly. Trench lines and barbed-wire entanglements stretched from the North Sea to the Swiss frontier with little change for the next four years, as did roads deliberately blocked with felled trees, placing impassable obstacles in the path of wheeled vehicles. Despite this, a number of RNACD squadrons were retained behind the front for a while. However, the Duke of Westminster's squadron provided fire support in the mobile pill-box role at the battles of Neuve Chapelle in March 1915 and Ypres in May of the same year and, at the latter, the cars played an invaluable service when the German gas attack made the work of runners impossible. Being less affected, the car crews were able to deliver messages and pass urgent orders relating to the conduct of the battle.

This action was the last British armoured car operation on the Western Front until movement was restored in 1918. Elsewhere in the world, however, there remained wide open stretches of terrain in which the RNACD could operate. Prominent among these were the remaining provinces of the Ottoman Empire, including Gallipoli, Palestine, Syria and Mesopotamia (Iraq), as well as the German colonies in South West Africa (Namibia) and German East Africa (modern Tanzania).

Chapter 3

Out in the Far Blue Yonder

Throughout the nineteenth century Great Britain had provided a prop for the ailing Ottoman Empire but, thanks largely to the machinations of Kaiser Wilhelm II and his ministers, in the early twentieth century that role had been assumed by Imperial Germany. Wilhelm enjoyed projecting an image of himself as the champion of Islam and during his visits to the Middle East, including Jerusalem, had himself announced as Hadji Mohammed Guillermo, thereby suggesting that he had made the pilgrimage to Mecca – which would not have been allowed – and had adopted as an additional name that of the Prophet himself. His hosts, more interested in acquiring German money, German arms and German training for their army, politely indulged him and even encouraged their guest's grandiose designs for two inter-continental railways, namely the Berlin-Baghdad Railway and the Berlin-Cairo-Cape Railway. Inevitably, this deepening relationship caused serious alarm in the British Foreign and Colonial Offices. On 15 August 1914, while Turkey was still neutral, the Sultan's government informed the Royal Navy's mission that its services were no longer required. It left Constantinople a month later, its place being taken by German advisers. Turkey was then required to repay her debt and, at German insistence, closed the Dardanelles, thereby denying Russia her only warm-water supply route. In response, Russia declared war on Turkey on 2 November and, four days later, Britain and France, being already allied with Russia, declared war on Turkey. It goes without saying that Turkey, amply supplied with arms, munitions and advisers by Germany and Austria-Hungary, was capable of causing a great deal of trouble for her former ally throughout the Middle East.

The Suez Canal, Britain's Imperial lifeline, was an obvious target. In January 1915 a Turkish corps under the command of Djemal Bey left Beersheba in southern Palestine and embarked on a crossing of the Sinai desert with the object of causing large-scale damage to the canal's facilities and possibly even blocking the waterway with sunken ships. The Turks' progress was reported regularly by Nieuport floatplanes flying off the canal so that when they did mount a series of uncoordinated attacks on the canal they were shot to pieces by a blizzard of fire from prepared defences on the western bank and waiting Allied warships. Having sustained 2,000 casualties, Djemal retired slowly to Beersheba.

If this round had gone to the Allies, the next unquestionably went to the Turks. The Allied plan was to force the passage of the Dardanelles and land on the Gallipoli peninsula, thereby posing a direct threat to the security of Constantinople. Unfortunately, a series of preparatory naval bombardments not only failed to produce the required results but also warned the Turks of what was intended. The initial landings took place on 25 April 1915 but were not exploited. Consequently, the British, French, Australian and New Zealand troops remained penned in their bridgeheads. Four Rolls Royce armoured cars had been landed, but spent most of their time in dugouts to protect them from the enemy's shellfire. On the few occasions on which they did emerge, they faced the same trench warfare problems that had locked the Western Front in France and were only able to supply direct fire support. A second landing was made between 6 and 8 August yet, incredibly, this was not exploited either and was quickly sealed off. The fighting was bitter and costly to both sides. Clearly the campaign was going nowhere and the decision to evacuate was taken on 23 November. Brilliant staff work ensured that the Turks remained oblivious as to what was going on. Troops, heavy weapons and stores continued to be loaded until the night of 8/9 January 1916 when the last men filed out of the trenches and down to the waiting boats. The Allies sustained 252,000 casualties, while the Turks incurred 251,000, including 21,000 killed by disease. Nevertheless, there could be no disguising the fact that the campaign had been a complete failure. Naval losses had also been heavy and Winston Churchill, always an advocate of the operation, lost his position as First Lord of the Admiralty.

Simultaneously, the Constantinople war ministry had been making plans for an invasion of Egypt from Libya.

This, it was hoped, would provoke such a widespread rising that it would drive the British out of the Middle East forever. In fact, Italy's hold on her new colony was tenuous and confined to a narrow coastal strip that included the fortified ports of Tripoli and Benghazi. Only rarely did the Italians penetrate the desert hinterland to the south, and then only in strength. Libya was, in fact, the home of the Senussi, a warlike Muslim sect with little liking for the British and none at all for the Italians. Matters were brought to a head when a U-boat torpedoed and sank a British armed boarding vessel, HMS *Tara*. The submarine's commander towed the survivors' boats into the little port of Bardia, where they became prisoners of the Senussi. U-boats, in fact, had become regular visitors to the Libyan coastline, bringing with them small arms, machine guns, mountain artillery and Turkish instructors.

As soon as they were aware of the situation, the British authorities in Egypt requested the Grand Senussi, Said Ahmed, to release the prisoners. At first the Grand Senussi denied any knowledge of them, but under pressure admitted that they were being held at an undisclosed location which he was not at liberty to divulge as the prisoners had been left in his care by the Turks as hostages. He was actually under heavy pressure from the Turks, two of the recent arrivals having brought the Grand Senussi a flattering letter from the Sultan, together with gifts of gold. One Turkish officer, Nuri Bey, was the brother of Enver Pasha, the Ottoman Empire's War Minister, and the other, Ja'far Pasha, had received his military education in Germany. They pointed out that the sinking of the *Tara* proved that the Royal Navy no longer ruled the waves, and that the British had been decisively beaten at Gallipoli. Now, they pointed out, was the time for a Senussi invasion of Egypt, where the population would rise to welcome them and help to drive out the British. Said Ahmed needed no further encouragement and ordered his troops to march.

During the night of 17 November the garrison of the frontier post at Sollum beat off several attacks and was then brought out by steamer. The following day it was the turn of Sidi Barrani. This, too, was held, but many of the Egyptian coast guards deserted to the enemy and the remainder, now too few to offer an adequate resistance, marched along the coast road to Sidi Barrani, grossly exaggerating the size of the force that had attacked them.

Lieutenant General Sir John Maxwell, Commander-in-Chief of the British troops in Egypt, had very limited resources at his disposal. They included several Territorial infantry battalions and Yeomanry cavalry regiments, which he placed under the command of Major General A. Wallace and designated the Western Frontier Force, but the fact was that he had insufficient assets to drive out the Senussi and deal with an internal security crisis if one arose. Fortunately, he had a number of Rolls Royce armoured cars at his disposal, drawn from the RNACD's Nos. 3 and 4 Squadrons, including those recently returned from Gallipoli., which were formed into the Emergency Squadron RNACD. Wallace fought a number of successful holding actions west of Mersa Matruh, halting the Senussi advance, and during these the armoured cars must have come as a most unpleasant surprise to the Senussi. A few of the crews had fired their Maxims in Gallipoli and knew what to expect, but the drivers among the rest were in for an unpleasant experience of their own. Of course, with armoured warfare in its infancy, few could have predicted the shower of hot cartridge cases that fell inside the backs of their shirts, causing painful red weals on the skin against which they were trapped. However, experience is a great teacher and it was not long before spent-case ejector bags were being devised and clipped under the guns. The Emergency Squadron saw little fighting after this because the winter rains turned the going into a quagmire. Nevertheless, by the time it was relieved by the Duke of Westminster's squadron it had accumulated considerable desert experience and was sent up the Nile to Upper Egypt where Senussi bands were threatening the security of the river's left bank, having operated in the oases of El Kharga, Dakhala, Farafra and Baharia. In due course its cars, and those of its personnel who wished, were transferred to the Army, with the notable exception of one.

Meanwhile, the Duke's squadron was settling in and acclimatising itself. It gave the impression of being a gentleman's motoring club which in one sense it was, the Duke having selected his officers and men with care. Most, including Second Lieutenant Griggs, his own jockey, were drawn from cavalry and yeomanry regiments, plus a number of professional motor drivers and mechanics. Among themselves, they referred to the Duke as Bendor, a Bend Or being the principal feature of his coat of arms.

In January 1916 air reconnaissance revealed that the Senussi had established an entrenched position at Halazin, some twenty-two miles south of Mersa Matruh. Wallace decided to eject them, but days of continuous rain had so soaked the desert that the cars could not be used. Instead, Wallace attempted to isolate the position with his cavalry, a move which was blocked by a counter-attack led by Ja'far. Despite this, the absence of the counter-attack force from the position was put to good use when the infantry drove the rest of the Senussi out of their trenches at bayonet point. The atrocious weather, in which the seriously wounded had to be carried for several miles, did nothing for Wallace's health and on 10 January he was relieved by Major General E. W. Peyton.

By now, reinforcements had begun to reach Egypt and these, plus troops recently withdrawn from Gallipoli, had increased the strength of the Western Frontier Force to the point that Maxwell ordered it to take the offensive and recapture Sollum. The enemy was now reported to be holding a position at a location called Agagya, some way to the south-east of Sidi Barrani. Peyton set out with a column consisting of two South African infantry battalions, the Dorset Yeomanry and one squadron of the Buckinghamshire Yeomanry, a Royal Horse Artillery battery and four of the Duke's cars. By the evening of 24 January the column had reached a point within eight miles of its objective. Peyton decided to rest his men and attack on the 26th.

The Senussi, some 1,500 strong, were found to be holding a ridge five miles north of Agagya and armed with machine guns and mountain artillery. Their fire started kicking up sand among the South African infantry as soon as they were within range and Ja'far sent out a counter-attack force to engage the British advance from a flank. This was defeated by a reserve that Peyton had formed with such a situation in mind. To the chagrin of the armoured car crews, their vehicles bogged down in soft sand, although they managed to provide continuous fire support for the attack with their dismounted machine guns emplaced on ground mountings. Eventually, after several hours of hard fighting, the Senussi began abandoning their trenches.

On the right of the British line the course of the action had been watched closely by Lieutenant Colonel Souter, commanding the Dorset Yeomanry. Once the Senussi were clear of their trenches he ordered his regiment forward. At once the enemy rearguard's machine guns opened up, cutting swathes through the ranks without slowing the momentum of the charge. The lines of galloping horsemen swept into the enemy mass, cutting down 300 of their opponents and chasing the rest far across the desert. At the very moment of contact Souter's horse was short dead beneath him and he was thrown, landing almost on top of Ja'far. The Turk, however, was wounded and, being in no position to resist, surrendered himself to Souter, commenting indignantly that in the prevailing circumstances the charge had been made contrary to the accepted tactical doctrine. True that may have been, but the results had been devastating, although the Dorsets' casualties (eighty-five men out of 184 present and eighty-five horses) had reduced the regiment's strength by half.

The next phase of the campaign saw Sidi Barrani occupied on 28 February. The advance was renewed on 9 March with the infantry and cavalry marching along the coastal route to Buq Buq and then swinging inland to climb the coastal escarpment near Augarin Wells. The Duke's cars, now at full strength, would climb the escarpment by means of a pass south of Sidi Barrani then advance parallel to the troops on the coastal plain below. In the event, the pass was more suited to animal transport than anything else, but all the cars reached the top after prodigious effort by the crews manhandling them over the worst stretches and fierce demands were made upon engines that produced clouds of steam from boiling radiators. The following day, heliograph contact was established with the infantry below, who signalled that the wells at Buq Buq were almost dry and that the water situation was becoming desperate. Some miles farther on the first South Africans reached the top of the escarpment, many with their tongues hanging out; one, a bank manager in civilian life, offered the then huge sum of £50 for a drink. There were no takers, for all that the armoured car crews had left was swilling about the bottom of their water bottles, and the contents of the vehicles' spare tanks had long been used to top up their radiators. The only other sources of water were in the radiators themselves or the machine guns' water-cooling jackets, and to touch either would result in a court martial. It was fortunate that the following morning the cars discovered a source of water, without which the advance could not have continued.

Halfaya Pass was reached on 14 March, as was Sollum, three miles beyond, indicating that the enemy had withdrawn from Egypt. This was confirmed by air reconnaissance, which also reported that the Senussi were now occupying a large encampment at Bir Wair, beyond the frontier. Peyton's force was now far removed from the supervision of General Headquarters in Cairo and Peyton was determined to destroy the Senussi field army before it could recover its strength and cause further trouble. He was not concerned that this would involve operations in Italian territory, as the Italians themselves seemed unwilling or unable to do anything about the menace, despite the fact that Italy had become Britain's ally the previous year. The Duke was summoned to his headquarters and given the most direct orders he could have wished for: he was to take his cars to Bir Wair and act with as much aggression as the situation commanded. The Duke could not have been more delighted. He was off the leash and free to deal with the situation as he thought fit.

Once across the frontier the going was found to be excellent and the cars were able to maintain a high average speed. Smoke on the distant horizon indicated the location of the Senussi camp but, as the cars closed in, it became apparent that this came from abandoned cooking fires. A brief reconnaissance discovered the Senussi themselves near a well named Bir Azeiz. They were occupying a boulder field behind an area of rough going and as the cars appeared they opened up on them with their machine guns and mountain artillery. The gunners manning the latter quickly learned the difficulties of ranging on a moving target with a low-velocity weapon and were unable to improve on a handful of near misses. The cars responded by fanning out and going for them, machine guns chattering. It quickly became unbearably hot inside the cars as the heat from the racing engines was added to that of the sun beating down on the armour plate. Added to this the choking fumes from the expended cartridge cases littering the turret floors turned the atmosphere blue. The noise level, a compound of roaring engine, the car's own machine gun firing, the rattle of the enemy's bullets striking, the shouts of the vehicle commander ordering changes of direction, came close to the level of intolerance. The cars were deliberately concentrating their fire on the enemy's artillery whose shells were passing overhead to explode well behind their intended target. The gunners themselves were mostly Turks and they stuck by their weapons until they were shot down around them. At this, the entire Senussi army broke and ran; some may have seen the cars in the distance during earlier engagements, but none had been attacked by them before and if the artillery was unable to halt then what chance had men with rifles? Hundreds were killed or wounded during the ensuing pursuit while others threw down their arms and surrendered. Nuri Bey himself came within an ace of being captured.

The engagement at Bir Azeiz should be seen as an important milestone in the history of armoured warfare. Just thirty-four men, protected by armour plate and with the superior mobility conferred by the internal combustion engine, had routed an entire army. The Duke's men sustained one or two slight injuries, almost certainly because of bullet-splash penetrating visors or interior flaking of armour under impact; some tyres had also been punctured. The squadron spent the night on the battlefield and returned to Sollum the following morning with its prisoners and captured weaponry, including three 4-inch guns, nine machine guns, numerous personal weapons and 250,000 rounds of ammunition. In recognition of its achievement the unit was paraded in front of the fort and commended by Peyton personally.

During the squadron's absence something remarkable had happened. A letter from Captain Gwatkin-Williams, the commander of the ill-fated *Tara*, had been discovered in a house in Sollum. It was addressed to the commander of the British garrison but had been delivered during the period of Senussi occupation. Nothing had been heard of the prisoners for many weeks, but the letter said that they were being held at a place named Bir Hackeim, also known as El Hakkim Abbyat. Neither name was entered on any of the maps, but it seemed possible that it was known to some of the prisoners. At first they were not forthcoming, but at length an elderly man named Ali said that in his youth he had tended stock there. Getting there would be a long journey, taking five days by camel, he said, adding that he would be prepared to act as guide.

The Duke then offered to lead a rescue attempt with his squadron. His offer was promptly accepted and a column was quickly assembled, including Ford tenders loaded with petrol, water and provisions, plus motor ambulances, a total of forty-five vehicles including the armoured cars. Leaving Sollum at 01.00 on 17 March, the column drove through the darkness through Bir Wair to Tobruk. After a short halt for breakfast the journey continued, now heading in a westerly direction. Soon after leaving Sollum, Ali's sharp desert eyes picked out a camel caravan moving along a parallel route to the south. It was intercepted by the armoured cars and found to contain supplies destined for the Senussi. These were confiscated, the drivers made prisoner and the camels shot. All this took longer than had been allowed for and it was noon before the column moved off again. Ali insisted that they carry on to the west and gave no further instructions. Anxieties were expressed concerning the amount of petrol that was being consumed and the Duke's interpreter pointed out to Ali that motor vehicles were unlike camels and had to be fed regularly. Ali passed no comment other than to repeat that this was the way to Bir Hackeim.

After 100 miles had been covered, Ali indicated that the column should swing left and head south over the desert. Most men began to feel uneasy if not a little fearful. They were heading away from everything familiar and into an unknown world. There was only the sky and the desert on which nothing moved save the occasional dust devil, rising without warning, revolving slowly and then collapsing. Had they come too far? At 15.00 the cars' milometers showed that they had covered 120 miles while their fuel gauges indicated that the column had reached the point of no return. By now the Duke, having completely lost confidence in Ali, ordered a halt to verify the column's position. At this point, Ali shouted that he could see Bir Hackeim. Through his binoculars the Duke could see two small hummocks rising from the desert floor and Ali assured him that the wells were underneath them.

As the cars fanned out to converge on the objective, armed men could be seen running away into the desert, taking their families with them. Next, skeletal, half-naked figures appeared, waving and cheering in cracked voices, tears flooding from staring eyes set deep in skull-like heads. It was difficult to realise that they had once been British seamen in the prime of life. Gwatkin-Williams was in better shape than his men, but even he had lost six stone in weight. He said that four men had already died of starvation, adding that their captors had shared their rations with them but there was never enough to go round and the seamen had been reduced to eating desert snails and roots. The Duke's medical officer confirmed that a fifth man was beyond saving and had only hours to live. The armoured car crews, blind with rage that the Senussi field army could feed itself yet leave its helpless prisoners to die of starvation, roared off in pursuit of the former guards. When they returned, silent, grim-faced and bitterly regretting that they had allowed their rage to get the better of them, they brought with them two babies that were the only survivors of their families. There can be no denying that this was a stain on an otherwise finely-executed operation.

As soon as the seamen had been clothed and fed, the column set out on the return journey, reaching Bir Wair, now held by part of the Australian Camel Corps, at 23.00. Most drivers, exhausted, fell into an instant sleep across their wheels. Worst affected were the armoured car drivers, as their seat consisted of a pile of mats and a strip of slung canvas for a back-rest. Meanwhile, the Duke had gone ahead to make arrangements for the former captives, who were embarked on a hospital ship for passage to Alexandria as soon as they reached Sollum. The cars had to remain at Bir Wair for two days before they could return to Sollum, where they were greeted by the cheers of the infantry, an artillery salute and the congratulations of General Peyton.

A more relaxed period followed. During this the squadron's sub-units took turns patrolling the 150-miles stretch of coast road between Mersa Matruh and Sollum. By now the Italians had begun to take an interest in the war and had established a fortified post of their own at Bardia. They had acquired accurate intelligence to the effect that Nuri Bey had rallied some of the Senussi and established a camp in the Wadi Saal, which ran down to the sea somewhere between Bardia and Tobruk. The decision was taken to mount a joint operation with the Italians, to flush the enemy out of this position, which was also a major delivery point for supplies landed from U-boats. This took place on 26 July. While the squadron's Rolls Royces lined both sides of the wadi, the Australian Camel Corps and the Italians, who were equipped with a number of light Fiat cars each mounting a machine gun, fought their way down it from the top, supported by the gunfire of a Royal Navy monitor lying offshore. After a sharp fight the Senussi broke and escaped down the wadi to the shore, led by Nuri Bey on his piebald horse. The various caves in the sides of the wadi were closed by stout wooden doors that were prised open, revealing a treasure trove of munitions and military stores that would have enabled the Senussi to renew their campaign for a considerable period.

This action virtually ended Senussi activity in the Western Desert, but Said Ahmed and his followers still continued to pose a threat to Upper Egypt and still regarded themselves as being completely secure in their fastness in the Qattara Depression where the oases of Siwa, Girba and Jarabub were situated in a valley 1,000 feet below sea level that could only be reached by descending a difficult escarpment some 200 miles south of Mersa Matruh. In summer, furnace heat accompanied by high humidity rendered it unpleasant if fertile, added to which it was a breeding ground for the malaria mosquito. No army had ever dared to penetrate this far into the desert, and perhaps the Senussi should have remembered that the internal combustion engine had given the British the power to do so. Furthermore, they were intent on applying it.

A force for the task was assembled at Sheka, 185 miles south of Mersa Matruh, under the command of Brigadier General Hodgson. It consisted of the Duke of Westminster's armoured car squadron and three light car patrols equipped with Model T Fords mounting a Lewis gun. On 3 February 1917 it set out to force the difficult pass leading to Girba while a flanking patrol covered the approach from Jarabub. The main body continued to descend slowly between barren hills and numerous re-entrants in an apparently deserted landscape. Suddenly the leading cars came under heavy small-arms fire and the advance halted for the night.

The following morning the cars pushed on past the site of the previous day's ambush, only to find the track littered with all kinds of obstacles. Constant work with picks, shovels and crowbars ahead of the cars was necessary simply to keep them crawling along at a snail's pace. After some hours of this the leading car was rounding a bend when the bang of a gun being fired was followed almost at once by a shell bursting on the cliff face above it. Rocks came thundering down until the vehicle was half buried. Needless to say, the crew wasted no time in racing for safety.

The Senussi gun crew must have been dozing, for two more cars reached the scene, attached their tow ropes and pulled the trapped car free with manual assistance. Suddenly the gunners awoke and sent a round into the very place from which it had been rescued. It was, however, clear that the gun must be neutralised before further progress could be made. With considerable difficulty two men climbed the cliff and hauled a machine gun after them. A Ford was sent round the bend to draw fire, which it did successfully, and the machine gun opened fire at the tell-tale flash of the enemy weapon, the crew of which ran off, abandoning it.

As the cars emerged from the pass at the foot of the escarpment they came under fire from every direction. It was almost impossible to locate the Senussi riflemen and the fight raged for the rest of the day without result. At dusk the cars withdrew into leaguer to replenish their ammunition and replace damaged tyres. When they renewed their attack the following morning it was evident that the Senussi were far from keen to renew the contest. Most had disappeared in the direction of Jarabub and the rest were quickly dispersed. As the cars advanced along the valley their crews entered a scene straight out of their imaginings of the Arabian Nights. Mile after mile of palms and avenues of fruit trees stretched away to the east while lakes of clear, fresh water sparkled in the sunlight. Never having seen a motor vehicle before, the inhabitants either stood rooted to the spot in amazement or ran in horror to hide themselves. The operation finally broke the power of Said Ahmed, who accepted the demands of his disgruntled followers and abdicated in favour of his less belligerent and more acceptable cousin Said Idris. This was the last operation to be carried out by the Duke's squadron. Before returning to the high desert and the greater war the crews were entertained to a sumptuous banquet by the local sheik.

While the armoured cars had, for the moment, left the Western Desert, their place was taken by Light Car Patrols. As well as monitoring the activities of the now quiescent Senussi, they provided the Army with the detailed maps that were used during the Second World War. Equally important, they conquered the natural unease felt by those new to the immense areas of emptiness that made up the wide blue yonder. The desert, they recognised, must always be respected and never taken for granted. With this in mind they established a set of desert-wise principles that hold good to this day. Good navigation was essential and, once chosen, no variation was permitted. A team of fitters and recovery specialists accompanied each patrol in the manner of modern Light Aid Detachments. For emergency use, air recognition panels were carried, as were sand mats, spades and at least two spare wheels per vehicle. Adequate margins of water and petrol were always allowed for. At this period, cooling systems were not pressurised and boiling was the norm rather than the exception. In such circumstances, the vehicles had the prior claim on the available water and, if necessary, the men were expected to go thirsty.

Lieutenant G. W. Richards joined the Duke's squadron shortly after the rescue of the *Tara*'s survivors and later transferred to a light car patrol. His travels took him as far south as Siwa and as far west as Bardia in Libya. They also took him to Bir Hackeim, little imagining that twenty-five years later he would command an armoured brigade in that very place.

Chapter 4

Outwitting an Admiral,
and a Few Generals Too ...

Oliver Locker Lampson MP was born into a wealthy family. Anyone who shopped in any department store worth the name would have been aware of the Lampson tube system. To complete one's purchase, the assistant would place his bill and the customer's money in a cylinder which he placed inside a pneumatic tube transporter. After a tortuous journey it arrived at a secure office in the bowels of the store where a lady removed the contents, receipted the bill which she enclosed in the cylinder with any change due, and sent it back to its point of origin. Retail organisations were not the only people to use the Lampson system. Large organisations with the need to maintain contact between distant departments also used it, so that it could also be used as a sort of contemporary internal e-mail.

Oliver's mother was an American by birth and settled to married life in England very well, with three dislikes that she passed on to her son. The first was tramps, whom she regarded as fiends whose only purpose in life was to attack honest citizens; the second was mad dogs, who had similar inclinations; and the third was copper coinage, which she was convinced carried all the infections of their previous users. The first she dealt with by supplying Oliver with a revolver which he took to Eton, where it miraculously escaped detection and which he continued to carry with him on his country walks in old age without encountering hostility from either tramps or mad dogs. She was able to enforce the ban on copper coins only while he remained in her care. He inherited from her the essence of American business methods, including the ability to arrange affairs to his own advantage. He was fond of both his parents, although, like Winston Churchill, it was for his nanny that he felt the greatest affection.

After leaving Eton he went to Cambridge and emerged with a degree in law. For a while he worked in the chambers of Mr Justice Bingham (later Lord Mersey) but developed an interest in politics and in 1907 was adopted as prospective Unionist candidate for the constituency of North Huntingdonshire. A popular figure, he won the seat from its Liberal member in the General Election of 1910. He enjoyed the life of a politician but still felt that something was lacking. That something appeared shortly after the outbreak of war in 1914. There always had been a glamour about the Royal Navy and when the RNACD began parading their armoured cars, flying the White Ensign, around the country as they sought suitable recruits, he knew that this was it. It was not just the sense of adventure that it offered, for he realised at once that if, like the Duke of Westminster, he could raise his own squadron, his activities would be regularly reported to his constituents.

It cost approximately £30,000, an enormous sum in 1914, to raise a squadron. He recruited men from the area of Cromer, close to his family home, and elsewhere in Norfolk, from Huntingdon and from his London acquaintances, but it was not enough. Fortunately, luck was on his side. Shortly before the outbreak of war the Home Rule Act had polarised opinion in Ireland to the extent that a civil war seemed likely. Fortunately, both sides agreed to put aside their differences until after the war. The Ulster Volunteer Force had strong ties with Locker Lampson's Unionist Party and in a gesture of loyalty to the crown it made good his shortage in money and men in conditions of the greatest secrecy. His squadron (No. 15) was now an established fact and he was appointed to lead it with the rank of commander.

Unfortunately, by the time it reached France the front was locked solid and set to continue that way. No. 15 Squadron was sent to the Belgian sector but there was little or nothing for it or any of the other RNACD squadrons present to do. This incurred the wrath of the Fourth Sea Lord, Commodore Cecil Foley Lambert, within whose sphere of responsibility the RNAS lay. He was now sharply critical of the RNACD.

> These officers and men are not pulling their proper weight in the war. If I had my way I would disband the whole lot of them. Anyhow, I am going to do my best to see that it is done and stop all this armoured car and caterpillar landship nonsense.

The 'caterpillar landships' were, of course, tanks, and while No. 20 Squadron RNACD was permitted to see their development through to the trials phase, Lambert more or less got his way with most of the remaining squadrons, which became part of the Machine Gun Corps. Others, like the Duke of Westminster's squadron, left for Egypt at the end of the year without making the change, as did elements of other squadrons already serving in different parts of the world.

Naturally this change in the fortunes of the RNACD upset Locker Lampson's plans. It was one thing to be the dashing commander of a naval armoured car squadron whose actions would be regularly reported to the electorate, and quite another to be submerged in the mass of an expanding organisation like the Machine Gun Corps which would, by its very nature, be confined to a supportive role. Luck, however, was on his side. To demonstrate their solidarity, several of the Allied nations had sent contingents to fight in each other's armies, and a Russian brigade was already serving in France. One evening Locker Lampson found himself dining with a senior Russian officer from the Paris military attaché's office and the conversation turned to the Belgians who, finding no further use for their armoured cars in the West, had formed a squadron which had been sent to Russia. The Eastern Front, explained the Russian, offered far greater scope for armoured car operations than the Western, and Russia was buying all the armoured cars she could lay her hands on, and had already placed large orders with Austins and other companies. Why, he asked, did not Locker Lampson volunteer his squadron for service with the armies of the Tsar? The idea had huge appeal for Locker Lampson. The very fact of a tiny handful of British men and machines fighting in an alien environment would generate a flow of publicity quite beyond its relative importance. He asked the Russian to put his request in writing, which he did, and upon its receipt he submitted a formal request for his squadron to be transferred to Russia.

In normal circumstances any such idea would have been dismissed out of hand, but following the Royal Navy's failure to force the Dardanelles and re-open Russia's only warm-water lifeline, followed by the disastrous Gallipoli campaign, any request from Russia had to be treated seriously. It was pointed out that the appearance of Locker Lampson and his cars in Russia would confirm that the Royal Navy still had a very long reach. Discussions between the Admiralty and the Russian Imperial General Headquarters (STAVKA) resulted in an agreement that the Admiralty would supply the vehicles and personnel while the Russians would pay all expenses, including pay at existing rates. Commodore Lambert was hardly in a position to argue.

Locker Lampson had struck gold. Instead of a single squadron he was to command a much larger force formed in the United Kingdom in October 1915. This consisted of three new squadrons numbered 1, 2 and 3, formed from the existing Nos. 15 and 17 Squadrons and reinforcements. Its fighting element included one Rolls Royce, thirty-three Lanchesters and five Pierce-Arrow heavies. During its formation and kitting out phase the unit was given the codename of President II, changed to the Russian Armoured Car Division (RACD) once it had become active.

On 4 December the unit sailed from Liverpool aboard the SS *Umona*. The following day she ran into the worst winter gale that her commander, Captain H. S. Robertson, could remember in twenty-five years at sea. At one point, three gigantic waves in succession laid the ship on her beam end for almost a full minute, during which the sound of crashing from the holds indicated that some of the armoured cars had broken loose. Those on the bridge clung to whatever they could, beginning to doubt whether the ship could ever pick herself up. She did, very slowly, shedding hundreds of tons of water. In the holds, the crashing continued as she righted herself, indicating the probability that many of the vehicles would require heavy repairs once ashore.

On the 8th the gale began to abate. *Umona* rounded the North Cape and put in to a small bay where her crew began to effect repairs. Midwinter darkness shrouded everything save for thirty minutes at noon, the compensation being that the men could stare in wonder at the flickering Aurora Borealis. The cold was beyond anyone's experience and coated the ship in ice. A message was received from the Senior British Naval Officer at Archangel to the effect that because of a winter of unusual severity the White Sea had frozen over and *Umona* stood no chance at all of getting through. During the gale two of the ship's lifeboats had been swept away. One had been discovered by another vessel and reported to the Admiralty, who were anxious to establish the ship's safety and, being aware of the conditions in the White Sea, sent a signal ordering her to return home and try to get through again in the spring.

Locker Lampson was horrified. He knew enough of service life to know that it was unlikely a second attempt would be permitted. Again, luck was on his side. *Umona* was to have been provisioned for just twelve days but a mistake had resulted in her carrying two months' provisions for everyone. That would enable her to sit out the winter until the spring thaw, when she would almost certainly be able to get through. If unsupported by any other reason, that would almost certainly not be acceptable to Their Lordships. Locker Lampson therefore sought the assistance of his senior medical officer, Surgeon Commander Scott. One or two of the men were suffering from pneumonia and he prompted Scott into agreeing that further exposure to the conditions current in the ship's hold could lead to an epidemic and in these circumstance he recommended that the men should be housed ashore in the ice-free port of Alexandrovsk where those affected could receive the necessary treatment in warm, restful conditions. On such matters, Scott's word was law and the Admiralty had to accept his recommendations. In fact, both officers were guilty of flagrant disobedience and plotting to deceive their superiors. The interesting thing is that the sick berth attendants knew exactly what was going on, but such was their regard for Locker Lampson that it would be sixty years before any of them spoke of it to anyone other than their immediate families.

Captain Robertson conned the *Umona* into Kola Inlet and the unit disembarked at Alexandrovsk. It was housed in wooden hutments that included stoves. A shipment of 6,000 rifles for the Russian Army had also been landed from another vessel. These would normally have been shipped south along a railway that was being constructed to the port through the frozen, heavily forested wilderness. The labour force consisted of German and Austro–Hungarian prisoners of war who were dying in scores daily because of overwork and inadequate clothing for the Russian winter. Consequently, the railway was falling steadily behind schedule. An officer of the Imperial Navy had arranged for reindeer trains to start moving the consignment but their progress was slowed because their route took them round a large frozen lake, adding many miles to their journey. A desperate officer of the Imperial Navy called on Locker Lampson requesting the unit's assistance. The transport echelon was detailed for the task and managed to cross the deeply frozen ice without difficulty, delivering its loads in a fraction of the time previously taken.

The rest of the unit continued to repair the damaged armoured cars. An indent for a large quantity of expensive spares was despatched. Considering that the unit had never been in action, this was not welcomed by the Admiralty and, with spring approaching, Locker Lampson knew that the pneumonia reason for remaining in Lappland would not hold good for much longer. He also received a warning, probably from Winston Churchill, warning him that senior officers at the Admiralty had again raised the subject of the unit's recall. The services it was performing for the Alexandrovsk port authorities were not producing an adequate return on their investment and could easily be carried out by men who were not trained armoured car crews. The matter had been discussed with the Russians who said they now had sufficient armoured cars of their own, adding that the Belgian squadron had failed to settle down. STAVKA did not wish to repeat the experiment and would raise no objections to the recall of the British unit.

Locker Lampson was horrified, but he still had one card to play and it would be very difficult for his opponents to trump it. It was a personal letter from King George V to the Tsar and Locker Lampson had been requested to deliver it personally. He left Alexandrovsk on 25 January 1916, travelling by ship to Norway, thence by way of Sweden to Petrograd, as St Petersburg was known during the war, and finally by rail to Mogilev, where Tsar Nicholas had his headquarters with STAVKA.

It was a fortnight before he was granted an audience with the Tsar. It was said that Locker Lampson could charm the birds from the trees and he certainly had engaging powers of persuasion. He pointed out to Nicholas that his men were already on Russian soil and were looking forward to fighting alongside the Russian Army, requesting that STAVKA should do everything possible to speed their journey to the front. He received the impression that he had won his point with an ease that surprised him. Later, as a further mark of Imperial favour, he was twice invited to eat with the Tsar and his personal staff. Incredibly, he had outflanked both the Admiralty and STAVKA at a stroke.

He returned to England via Sweden and Norway and in the middle of April boarded the *Umona* once more for his return to Alexandrovsk. She sailed in company with two Russian liners, the *Czar* and the *Dvinsk*, aboard which were new armoured cars to replace those damaged beyond repair during the winter gale, as well as other vehicles. When the convoy dropped anchor in the Kola inlet on 22 April, Locker Lampson found Alexandrovsk to be almost free of its canopy of Arctic snow. The unit's morale was good, but its embarkation for Archangel was being delayed by the need to provide guards and medical care for 1,000 exhausted prisoners of war sent north from the railhead for trans-shipment to Archangel. Locker-Lampson, by now thoroughly restless, decided to make his own way to Archangel via Norway, Sweden and the main railway line north from Petrograd, narrowly escaping arrest as a spy on the way.

When news of the rebellion in Dublin reached Alexandrovsk shortly after the event, the Irishmen aboard, Catholic and Protestant alike, were understandably concerned for the safety of their families. They demanded instant repatriation and, when illegally-hoarded rum inflamed the situation, threatened to take over the *Umona* and sail her to Ireland themselves. With the situation now dangerously out of control, Commander Gregory summoned Marines from British warships anchored in the Kola inlet. The arrival of these, coupled with the consumption of the last drops of alcohol, restored calm, but when *Umona* sailed for England she had aboard the ringleaders from both factions, some professional malcontents and a handful of serious medical cases, a total of thirty-one men. On 23 May the RACD personnel embarked on board the *Czar* while the prisoners of war boarded the *Dvinsk*. Late ice caused some further delay as the ships headed south across the White Sea, but the ships docked at Archangel five days later.

On 1 June the unit boarded a train for an interminably long journey south to Moscow, which was finally reached at 01.30 on 5 June. At every major station along the way the new arrivals had been cheered, bands had played and important local dignitaries had made speeches of welcome. However, the welcome in Moscow exceeded all expectations and even produced some unexpected humour. As the men left their carriages in an attempt to fall in on the platform a band struck up the British National Anthem. Naturally, the men stood to attention and their officers saluted. At every attempt to fall in, the band struck up another verse, including (latterly) several whose existence came as a complete surprise. It took thirty minutes for the RNAS men to form ranks, after which the parade commander said a few words of welcome and everyone was sent back to bed.

Locker Lampson and his officers were summoned to the Kremlin next day and, in the absence of the Imperial Family, were formally received by the Grand Duchess Elizabeth, sister of the Tsarina, and presented with suitable mementoes of the occasion. Some time later, Locker Lampson received his orders. These had been drafted by STAVKA, which had not enjoyed being outwitted by a comparatively junior officer and had decided to send the British unit to Transcaucasia, hundreds of miles to the south, to assist in controlling the indigent Kurds and keeping the Turkish Army out of southern Russia. It was actually a sensible decision as the area resembled the North West Frontier of India, on which the British were involved in a semi-permanent state of hostility with the local tribes, although it seems to have been forgotten that none of the RNAS personnel had ever been near the place. Very few people at home would be aware that fighting was going on in Transcaucasia because it was so rarely in the news that British reporters hardly ever visited it. All in all, it seemed probable that he would disappear completely, thanks to STAVKA having turned the tables on him. However, an order was an order and had to be obeyed.

The first phase of what would prove to be yet another long journey would take the unit as far as Vladikavkaz in the Caucasus, where it was comfortably accommodated in one of the Imperial Army's military academies. Of its armoured cars and lorries, which had last been seen on their flats in a siding at Archangel there was no sign. The weeks came and went until, in desperation, Locker Lampson reported the matter to the local area commander. Things then started to happen, but in the wrong order. The unit was presented with a mascot in the form of an engaging little black bear named Miska. Unfortunately, in a frighteningly short space of time Miska grew into a large, ill-tempered bear who showed signs of wanting to eat his keeper, Petty Officer Spencer, and had to be sent the way of all bad bears. Then, at last, the vehicles arrived. The guards who travelled with them hadn't the faintest idea where they had been as one siding looks very like another and it was difficult to interpret the Cyrillic script in which the station name-boards were written. However, they knew that they must be approaching their destination as the temperature grew steadily warmer and flora and fauna more exotic and colourful.

Having disembarked the vehicles from their flats and checked them over, the unit set off for Transcaucasia through some of the most difficult country in the world. Sometimes the track amounted to nothing more than a ledge, barely wide enough for the vehicles, with a towering mountainside on one side and a drop of many hundreds of feet on the other. An advance guard of Cossacks led the way, persuading travellers travelling in the opposite direction to turn round or have their vehicles thrown off the cliff. At other times the road, while marked as being suitable for motor transport, was little more than a bridleway. There were fords of uncertain depth to be negotiated and bridges of doubtful strength to be crossed. On one occasion a wooden bridge clearly marked on the map had been broken up by the Cossacks guarding it simply to keep themselves warm at night. On another a Lanchester sustained a breakdown that was beyond the crew's ability to repair, although they managed to persuade a farmer to tow it several miles into the unit's night leaguer, using his two oxen. Their arrival caused much mirth although Locker Lampson was not amused, feeling, without too much cause that the unit's reputation had been compromised.

The unit reached Tiflis on 31 July but was unable to proceed further because incessant rain had washed out the road. The vehicles were therefore loaded onto railway flats and reached the ancient city of Kars the following day and arrived in Sarikamish on 3 August. The following day it was inspected by the Grand Duke Nicholas Nikolaievich, the Viceroy of the Caucasus and uncle of the Tsar.

A few days later Locker Lampson travelled to Erzerum and paid his respects to General Nikolai Yudenich, under whose command his unit would be fighting. Erzerum, like the rest of the Transcaucasian Front, actually lay within the Turkish hinterland in Asia Minor. In 1914 Enver Pasha had launched a major Turkish invasion of the Caucasus. This subsequently acquired the reputation of being the worst planned and conducted campaign in history. The Turks were thrown back and endured hideous loss of life as they withdrew through the heavy winter snow in the mountains. More recently they had tried to recover some of the lost ground with a counter-offensive but had been roundly defeated by Yudenich at Sarikamish. Now, the view of the general was that there was very little left for the cars to do, although the Kurds would probably give trouble and be assisted by the Turks in doing so. In the circumstances, he continued, there was no point in keeping the British unit concentrated. No. 1 Squadron, under Lieutenant Commander Belt, was to cover the right flank of the Russian troops that had been deployed defensively in North Persia, and operate south of Lake Urmia. The remainder would operate on his own army's open left flank, crossing the Mush Plain to Bitlis and supporting the Cossack cavalry units that held an ill-defined line as far as Lake Van. Finally, Yudenich emphasised, the British squadrons could expect no logistic support from the Russians and would have to carry all their own ammunition, food and petrol.

Over 350 miles separated Sarikamish from Bitlis, most of it through difficult and dangerous country inhabited by actively hostile Kurds. Inevitably, unarmoured vehicles required an armoured escort, which limited the number of fighting vehicles that could be employed at the front. It was therefore decided that No. 3 Squadron, under Locker Lampson's personal command, would operate forward and be supplied by Commander Gregory's No. 2 Squadron, operating from a forward base located at the isolated bridge at Keupri Keui.

Locker Lampson's squadron had not even established itself at its new base when it was forced to fight its way through an ambush involving a substantial number of Kurds. Some days later, one of the Heavies bogged down in a ford. After sending the rest of the squadron on, the commander returned with his tourer and one Lanchester to render assistance. It was clear that the Heavy could be freed by digging a channel to divert the water round the car, but after two hours work it was apparent that more time was required. Locker Lampson decided to leave the two armoured cars and rejoin the rest of the squadron.

After a while the tourer entered a narrow track running between low hills. Suddenly a heavy fire was opened on it, kicking up the dust all round. Lacking any sort of protection, it seemed as though survival of the vehicle would be a miracle. The driver, Petty Officer Weller, was maintaining the best possible speed, given the pitted nature of the going, while Locker Lampson, his orderly and a Cossack guide returned the fire as best they could. Nevertheless, the outlook remained bleak until Locker Lampson decided to employ his last and completely unexpected resource. He had fitted the Rolls with a horn that wound its way to a snake's head that produced such a horrendous volume of noise that no constabulary in the United Kingdom would have tolerated it.

'Sound your klaxon!' he shouted to Weller.

A deafening brassy bellow filled the valley, suggesting that the devil's own trumpeter was summoning all the cavalry in hell. The firing stopped as the Kurds prepared to meet their imagined assailants. At least two minutes elapsed before it was resumed and by then their aim had been seriously disturbed. The car rounded a bend only to discover a river stretching across the track some 300 yards ahead. It was apparent that, if depth of the water was too great, everyone aboard would have to swim for it, but there could be no turning back and in the event it was never more than fifteen inches deep. Half a mile beyond a Lanchester appeared and then the remainder of the squadron, which, under Lieutenant Commander Sholl, had beaten off a heavy attack themselves. The lorries were riddled but had been protected from the worst of enemy fire by deploying the armoured cars around them. Several men and one officer had sustained minor wounds, but everyone was astonished that the occupants of the Rolls tourer had survived at all. 'You have shaken Death by the beard!' was the verdict of one of the Cossack escort. During the evening the two missing cars came in.

A base was established without difficulty at a location that became known as Happy Valley. Shortly after the divisional intelligence staff warned that the Turks were planning a major attack and suggested that the base should be abandoned, along with such vehicles as were under repair. Locker Lampson would have none of it and was determined to go over to the offensive. This was easier said than done as the fuel supply was dangerously low. The problem was overcome by rationing whatever was available so that the armoured cars had a range of twenty miles. This was used to carry out a detailed reconnaissance of Turkish positions around the plain in such a manner that the enemy believed that they were to be attacked. A day or two later Commander Gregory brought up a supply convoy, escorted by armoured cars from No. 2 Squadron which kept the inevitable snipers at a distance.

Locker Lampson was now itching for action and entered detailed planning with the Russians, who were willing to supply troops and lay on a diversionary artillery barrage elsewhere along the line. The initial objective was a village occupying the entrance to a valley that led into the heart of the enemy's rear areas. Unfortunately, Locker Lampson does not name the village in the article he wrote for *Lloyd's Magazine*, but he does comment that halfway between Happy Valley and the objective lay a large circular tower and other ruins, close to a pool some 300 yards in diameter which provided the source of three streams flowing away in different directions, and this might help to identify the location.

During the night prior to the attack the cars moved up to the ruins, which provided cover from view, while on the left a joint British/Russian mounted force with Maxims carried on horseback entered a gully that would take them into the village without being seen. H-hour coincided with first light. 'In five minutes (the cars) were level with the tower,' wrote Locker Lampson, and the ceaseless chattering of the Maxims rolled over the hills. The village had not realised its danger until one car was only 600 yards away; and then it was as if someone had lifted a stone from it, exposing black insects in an agony of commotion. From the huts, the houses, the barns, tiny figures of men shot out until the terraces and fields were crawling with battalions in flight. There seemed no organisation or rallying point. A few tried the road up the valley, some scrambled painfully up the mountainside and I distinctly heard the Maxims of Turner's horsemen in the gully beating back the escape that way.

The village, set ablaze by the Heavies' 3-pounders, was taken without difficulty, which also dispersed several groups of the enemy attempting to rally on the high ground. Prisoners confirmed that another village 4,000 yards up the valley contained the headquarters of two infantry battalions and an ammunition dump. It was difficult to get a view of it from the entrance to the valley, but the tops of some poplar trees suggested its position. Taking these as his aiming mark, Chief Petty Officer Benson crept up on the target by elevating his 3-pounder with every shot. Six shells crossed the intervening crest without result, but when the seventh, followed rapidly by the eighth hit the target, two huge explosions seemed to shake the hills and create a blast wave. It was subsequently learned from prisoners that a magazine and ammunition dump had exploded almost simultaneously, killing in excess of 300 Turks. The exact date of this engagement remains unknown, but PO Baker of No. 2 Squadron heard of it on 27 August and entered details in his diary, so it can only have taken place a day or so earlier. Naturally, the Russians were delighted with the outcome of the affair. The Grand Duke awarded the unit six St George's Crosses and eleven St George's Medals to be conferred on the men Locker Lampson considered to be the most deserving.

Autumn arrived early in this part of the world, where high altitude cold and deep mountain snow quickly made winter operations impossible. Then, at the beginning of October, Romania declared war on the Central Powers. Locker Lampson, seeing that no further opportunity for fighting would present itself on the Transcaucasian front for several months, travelled to the Grand Duke's headquarters in Tiflis and requested that his unit should be transferred to Romania, confident that this would provide a flow of favourable publicity for consumption by the British electorate. Nicholas, however, was not inclined to commit himself but provided Locker Lampson with a letter of introduction to General Michel Alexeiev, the Tsar's Chief of Staff. Locker Lampson therefore travelled to Imperial General Headquarters at Mogilev where, to his surprise, Alexeiev revealed that he had a poor opinion of the Romanian Army, predicting that it would quickly be trounced by the battle-hardened German and Austrian troops it would be facing, to say nothing of its ancient Bulgarian enemies. He did, however, suggest that if the British unit wanted fighting, he could send it to Galicia, where plenty of action was available. Seeing which way the wind was blowing, Locker Lampson suggested bringing the unit north to Odessa, midway between the two theatres of war, and then deploying it as circumstances demanded. This was agreed to and, after a second meeting with the Tsar, he left for England. The Grand Duke was informed of the decision and the necessary movement orders were issued by his British Military Attaché, Major Archibald Wavell of the Black Watch, who, the previous year, had lost an eye during the fighting at Ypres. In a future war he would win a series of resounding victories in North Africa and, later, become Viceroy of India.

Locker Lampson arrived in London bearing letters for King George V from the Tsar, the Grand Duke Nicholas and General Alexeiev and was no doubt thanked for his trouble. In other respects he does not seem to have enjoyed his visit and was absent from his command for no less than three months. No doubt Their Lordships of the Admiralty were glad to get their hands on him at last and had certainly not forgotten the sleight of hand by which he had reached Russia in the first place, then indulged in a well-publicised trip into Transcaucasia. Now, without so much as a by-your-leave, he had arranged for the transfer of a major unit of the Royal Navy from one theatre of war to another. He might be a Member of Parliament and something of a Royal postman, but for the moment his career was hanging by a thread. His request that the unit's Lanchesters should be replaced by Rolls Royce armoured cars was, to say the least, ill timed. Their Lordships' response was that they had already spent enough on his private army and were not prepared to spend any more. Just one area provided any cause for satisfaction. In the Caucasus Locker Lampson had noted that, because of their high ground clearance, the Model T Ford tenders had the best cross-country performance of all the vehicles present. The unit still possessed a home depot at Newport, Monmouthshire, and he ordered its personnel to produce an armoured version. The design produced by CPO L. Gutteridge consisted of an armoured cab for the driver behind which was an open-topped superstructure mounting a rear-facing Maxim, the crew of which were protected by a 9mm gunshield. A quick-release mechanism enabled the gun to be dismounted for ground use. The additional armour doubled the vehicle's weight but this was allowed for by strengthening the suspension. The project received official approval and nine were built by G. Allen and Sons of Tipton, Staffordshire, and these had already been despatched to Russia while Locker Lampson was on his way home.

The unit, under the temporary command of Commander Gregory, had by now assembled at Odessa, Nos. 2 and 3 Squadrons arriving on 31 October. No. 1 Squadron in northern Persia had seen no real fighting and its battles had been fought against an unhealthy climate and difficult terrain; having further to travel, it had not reached Odessa until 4 November. Thereafter, only routine signals were received in London. However, on Christmas Day 1916 the Duty Operator at the Admiralty took down the following signal from Russia;

BRITISH ARMOURED CARS UNDER MY COMMAND IN ACTION DECR 25TH IN ROMANIA FURTHER COMMUNICATIONS LATER ENDS. ACTING COMMANDER GREGORY

On Boxing Day a second signal was received:

BRITISH ARMOURED CAR DIVISION IN ACTION IN ROMANIA DECR 26TH STOP. NO CARS LOST STOP. CASUALTIES LIEUT LUCAS SHADWELL SLIGHTLY WOUNDED LIEUT SMILES SLIGHTLY WOUNDED OPERATIONS STILL PROCEEDING. ENDS.

It seems improbable that these two signals were shown to Locker Lampson before the holiday ended, but further signals continued to arrive in a steady stream.

FOLLOWING ADDITIONAL CASUALTIES BRITISH ARMOURED CAR DIVISION ROMANIA STOP. CPO MACFARLANE 2772 PO FEAR 2989 WOUNDED ENDS.

And

BRITISH ARMOURED CAR DIVISION CONTINUOUSLY IN ACTION ROMANIA STOP. REPORT LOSS ONE SMALL ARMOURED CAR DESTROYED TO PREVENT FALLING INTO ENEMY'S HANDS STOP. GUN SAVED. ENDS. NUMBER 534. ACTING COMMANDER GREGORY

Locker Lampson was horrified. He was well aware that any politician's bitterest enemies lie within his own party and that the fact that he had spent Christmas at home while his command was engaged in heavy and sustained fighting would certainly be used against him. Unless he could return to the front immediately his political and military career could be regarded as over. The question was, would the Admiralty let him go?

Chapter 5

Russian Roulette

In their respective views of the Romanian Army's efficiency General Alexeiev had been right and Commander Locker Lampson wrong. Anyone who knew anything about Romania was aware that its peasant soldiery was hardy enough and would do its duty to the best of its ability despite the raffish qualities of its fashionable society being mirrored in some quarters of its officer corps, to the extent that it had been considered necessary to issue a general order to the effect that officers below the rank of major were forbidden to use make-up. The RNAS personnel considered them to be little better than 'chocolate soldiers', which was perhaps a little harsh, although when push came to shove they preferred to fight alongside the tough, uncomplaining Russians in their drab uniforms.

In June the Russian army group commanded by General Alexei Brusilov had launched a surprise offensive on the south–western sector of the front. By September the opposing Austrians had been flung back as far as the Carpathian foothills and only the arrival of German troops drawn from the Western Front stabilised the situation. However, although the Imperial Russian Army had fought its most successful battle of the war it had sustained a terrible 550,000 casualties and was exhausted. Furthermore, Brusilov was embittered by the lack of support he had received from his fellow army group commanders and the failure of STAVKA to keep him supplied with food, munitions and reinforcements. His sympathies now lay firmly with the revolutionary movement.

In Bucharest, Prime Minister Bratianu the Younger could only see that the Brusilov had inflicted 700,000 casualties on the Austrians, who seemed to be on the verge of collapse. On 27 August he declared war on Austria and Germany and mounted an invasion of Transylvania. All went well for a while, but then the Germans arrived and threw them back over the border. Bratianu had not declared war on Bulgaria, his southern neighbour and had left only a thin screen of troops along their common frontier. Bulgaria, unfortunately, was allied with Germany and Austria. Her troops attacked on 1 September and advanced up the Black Sea coast, taking the vital port of Constanza on 22 October while simultaneously advancing down the Danube and into the Dobruja, containing the delta of the great river. For Russia, this was a disaster as she was forced to pour troops into this area to protect her southern flank, troops who were desperately needed elsewhere.

Gregory was ordered to have the unit ready to move at a moment's notice. On 14 November it left Odessa by rail, travelling through Bolgrad to reach Reni, where the vehicles were unloaded. Further progress towards the front was to have been made by road but continuous rain alternating with snow had rendered the going impossable. The cars were therefore loaded onto three enormous grain barges which were towed upstream by a paddle steamer, passing Galatz and Braila on 25 November and reaching Hirsova on the 27th. Gregory had actually travelled this route in 1907 for he was a qualified Danube pilot and had conned HMS *Barham* up the river as far as Galatz during a courtesy visit.

The unit went into action on 27 November and remained in almost constant contact with the enemy until 4 January 1917. During this period men and vehicles were both tested to the limit. Their opponents were Bulgarians of whose soldierly qualities they knew nothing. In the event they proved to be tough and determined fighters who would give nothing away without a struggle. At Hirsova the unit joined IV Siberian Corps and was absorbed into the plans for a spoiling attack drawn up by the corps' commander, Lieutenant General Sirelius. This, it was hoped, would drive the Bulgarians back towards Constanza and the important Danube crossing at Cernovada. The detailed plans required

Nos. 1 and 3 Squadrons, under respectively Lieutenant Commander Belt and Lieutenant Smiles, to support the attack at Topalul, fifteen miles to the south, while Lieutenant Commander Wells-Hood's No. 2 Squadron carried out a similar operation a little farther to the east, near the village of Pantelimon Ustin. The first of these attacks reached the enemy's wire and kept the Bulgarians pinned down in their trenches, but such was the weight of fire directed at the cars that, for the moment, a Russian infantry attack seemed out of the question. The cars themselves were withdrawn with difficulty and considerable risk because, while reversing to engage over their rear, they had run into soft ground and bogged down. In addition, shell splinters and return fire had penetrated their Maxims' cooling water jackets, putting the guns out of action. However, the fact was that the cars had pressed their attack with the result that the Russians managed to capture a hill on either flank from their weakened defenders.

Despite this, few of the British armoured car crews had ever witnessed an infantry attack at close quarters and they were horrified by what they saw. 'The Russians advanced from their trenches, being cut down in their hundreds, but it was not until the wounded came in that we realised the full horror of war,' wrote PO Baker. PO Martin was also shaken by what he had seen and clearly felt enormous sympathy for the Russian infantry.

They are a poor lot of men. They are Siberian regiments, some with no boots on their feet, and they look as though they have had no food for a week. They are very young, or old men. A party of us volunteered to help them with the wounded. As they came in in carts we carried them into the dressing rooms set up in old houses. I saw some awful sights. All the wounds were very dirty with shrapnel and bullets still in the flesh, the blood sticking the clothes to the wound. We carried them in, the nurses dressed them and then we carried them to tents and there laid them on straw.

At Topalul the unit's two doctors, Surgeon-Commander Scott and his brother Surgeon-Lieutenant Maitland Scott, had set up their own casualty clearing station. The wounded began arriving during the evening of 30 November and from that time onwards the two surgeons and their staff worked incessantly, dealing with 2,000 cases in twenty-four hours.

Over at Pantelimon Ustin No. 2 Squadron had gone into action on 1 December. Wells-Hood was one of the most experienced armoured car commanders in the RACD, having already seen action at Antwerp, in France, Belgium, South-West Africa and Turkey. To his delight, the enemy left their trenches and advanced towards his position, being under the impression that all the British cars were employed on the opposite flank. He let them come on until they were far ahead of their trenches and moving in the open, then broke cover with his cars when they were only sixty yards distant and opened fire. Some dived for cover but the vast majority turned and fled back towards their trenches. The cars followed along the road, mowing them down until the last had vanished from view. Wells-Hood ordered Lieutenants Mitchell and Ingle to leave the road at intervals of 150 yards and engage a portion of the trench lines that were not visible to him. Unfortunately, the going across country was atrocious and both cars bogged down. Their engines cut out and they were re-started manually despite increasingly heavy fire. Unfortunately, the tyres on both cars were ripped to shreds and, due to the additional effort required because of this and thick mud, the engines stalled again. Simultaneously, the Maxims' water jackets were torn open, so that the cars could neither move nor fight. Lieutenant Ingle dismounted twice to re-start his car's engine, but on neither occasion was the engine equal to the additional burdens put upon it. On the second occasion a bullet smashed his leg above the knee. After shouting for his men to take cover, he dropped into a shell hole and lost consciousness.

For the next hour the two Lanchesters were battered continuously by shellfire that half-smothered Ingle with soil and debris. At the end of this the Bulgarian infantry came out and, after glancing briefly at Ingle, made prisoners of both crews and marched them off. When Ingle came to he had an impression of a cloudless sky, further firing, the running of many feet and hoarse cries, then he slid into unconsciousness again. When he next came to it was dark. A searchlight was sweeping the battlefield and there was an occasional splutter of rifle fire. He was aware of the thud of hooves and muted voices. Looking over the edge of the shell hole, he could see men and horses working around Mitchell's car. His immediate thought was that they were Bulgarians and he remained quiet until they had gone.

A heavy frost had checked the bleeding from his wound and hardened the ground. He decided to try and reach the Russian lines, but the only way he could move was by placing his injured leg on top of his sound one and pushing himself along on his back, using his hands. Every ten minutes he was forced to rest and by first light was utterly exhausted and beginning to hallucinate. Glancing over his shoulder he saw that the Russian wire was only eighty yards away and used his remaining strength to shout a phrase taught to every man in the unit: 'I am an Englishman fighting for Russia and am wounded.' Minutes later came the sound of running feet and a sergeant with six men arrived to carry him in.

There the sounds that he had heard while semi-conscious were explained to him. Quite possibly at Wells-Hood's request, the commanding officer of the 39th Siberian Rifles had not only mounted a vigorous local counter-attack that had pushed the Bulgarians back for several hundred yards but also provided horse teams and a working party that had recovered the damaged cars after dusk under the direction of Lieutenant Hunter. They had done their work so well that Wells-Hood had recommended them for a decoration.

It is just possible that, on its own, Sirelius' spoiling attack might have succeeded in stabilising the Dobruja sector, despite the heavy casualties that had been incurred. Elsewhere, however, the Romanian army had been mauled beyond recovery at the Battle of the Arges

River and Bucharest itself had fallen to the enemy on 6 December. The developing situation therefore indicated that unless he initiated a rapid withdrawal to the north his corps would be trapped between the Bulgarians in the Dobruja and the Austro-German forces now advancing steadily eastwards that would soon be capable of bringing pressure to bear on his right flank. Gregory was summoned to the headquarters of the Russian Sixth Army, of which Sirelius' corps formed part, and received orders for his cars to cover the movement.

I arrived back at Hirsova at 10 p.m. on 8th December to find that orders had already been given for the evacuation of the town. Lieutenant-Commander Belt had acted very promptly, immediately commandeering two Romanian barges at the jetty and loading up all our stores, ammunition, repair staff, broken down cars, etc. One barge had already left for Reni by the time I arrived and the loading up of the second was proceeding rapidly. After reporting to the Chief of Staff of the IVth Siberian Corps I was ordered to take over the defence of Hirsova until its complete evacuation.

On 13 December he was ordered to abandon Hirsova and move to Alebei Choi. The move was completed by the morning of the 15th but the following day Gregory received a warning order from Sirelius to the effect that the cars were needed at Braila, fifty miles distant and on the opposite bank of the Danube, and that they should arrive there not later than the 19th. The unit's two Russian liaison officers, Lieutenants Lamkert and Reppmann, were sent off on a route reconnaissance, but whatever plans might have been made were rendered meaningless by a major Bulgarian breakthrough on the 17th. Gregory was watching his allies in disgust, regarding them as 'a rabble, blocking their own roads and completely disorganised', when a mounted staff officer galloped up with fresh orders for him. The unit was to proceed to Tulchea in the Danube delta, where barges would be available for its evacuation.

At 09.00 the whole force left Alebei Chioi and headed for Tulchea, arriving at 11.30 on 17 December. Confusion reigned within the town following the issue of orders that it was to be evacuated within forty-eight hours. Gregory's responsibilities were suddenly increased by an order placing the personnel and vehicles of the Scottish Women's Hospital, a privately sponsored organisation formed from volunteer nurses for service on the Eastern Front, under his protection. The situation required steady nerves and calm thinking, and fortunately Gregory possessed both.

I divided the force into three as follows:

1. All the light transport and touring cars under Lieutenant-Commander Belt, which I despatched at midnight by road to Isaksha to cross the pontoon bridge at that place and proceed to Bolgrad and await further orders from me.
2. All the heavy transport including two transport wagons belonging to the Scottish Women's Hospital with the attendant nurses, I placed on the barge proceeding to Ismail under Sub-Lieutenant Turner, with orders to proceed from Ismael to Bolgrad to join Lieutenant-Commander Belt, and await further orders from me.
3. All the fighting cars, ammunition, etc, I took under my command on board the cars with the Russian armoured cars and proceeded to Reni.

We were delayed 24 hours on the way up owing to the non-opening of the pontoon bridge at Isaksha of which refugees and troops were continually passing in an unending stream.

By the afternoon of 19 December the cars reached Reni. Gregory was seriously worried that the fighting near Hirsova and the wear and tear sustained during the withdrawal had reduced their efficiency to the extent that they would be unable to provide the Siberians with the necessary support when the unit rejoined them. It would, he felt, amount to something akin to a minor miracle if he could scrape together a single serviceable squadron. The minor miracle was actually waiting for him at Reni in the form of CPO Gutteridge, his converted Ford armoureds and the home rear party who had just completed their long rail journey from Archangel.

Although Gregory had been given Braila as his unit's final destination, he believed that the roads in that area were unfit for armoured car operations. In this he was supported by the commander of the Russian armoured cars, Captain Grabovoi, who indicated that he had already obtained permission for his detachment to withdraw to Odessa. Gregory, feeling that the national honour would be prejudiced if he withdrew without a further fight, issued orders for his unit and its water transport to be concentrated at Galatz before going into action. He also formed Special Service Squadron A, consisting of the two Heavies *Ulster* and *Londonderry*, six Ford armoureds, one Lanchester lorry, two Ford lorries and one Pierce Arrow heavy lorry, under the command of Lieutenant W. D. Smiles.

Despite reservations regarding the roads in the Braila area, Smiles and his squadron were sent there, almost certainly at the Russians' request. On 23 December he patrolled beyond the town without encountering the enemy, although he was able to confirm the vile condition of the roads. The next day he was directed to support the Russian 124th Division at Vizural, where the commander of its 2 Brigade, Colonel Balgramo, took him forward to point out a village named Roobla, believed to contain two artillery batteries and infantry. While they were talking, a shell from Roobla landed nearby, killing two Russians and slightly wounding Lieutenant Edwards and CPO MacFarlane. With Balgramo's approval, Smiles decided to shoot up the enemy village with his heavies at dawn next day.

The shoot was carried out on 25 December by Lieutenant Lucas Shadwell in *Ulster* with Sub-Lieutenant Henderson in *Londonderry* in reserve. Two houses, reputed to conceal the enemy's guns, were destroyed and the Russian outposts reported casualties and further damage in the village. The range was increased to engage a second village through which it was believed ran the main road. The dose was repeated the following day and seems to have enraged the Bulgarians who mounted a major attack as the two heavies were leaving Vizural. Smiles obtained the divisional commander's permission to bring up the rest of his cars and ordered the heavies to return to Vizural at once and cover the Roobla road. Simultaneously, Lieutenant Shadwell, now commanding a Ford armoured, was ordered to take the right fork in the village and engage the flank of the enemy's attack. Smiles, also in a Ford armoured, returned to the village to find Sub-Lieutenant MacDowell's two heavies banging away at the Bulgarians along the road.

'Don't fire unless you've got a target,' he shouted. 'The lorries are on their way up but don't waste a single round!'

He then took a road on the left, leading to the village of Perlita, where he came across Balgramo manning a field telephone in his command post. The Colonel told him that the Siberians had lost heavily and requested him to take his car out beyond the wire and hold off the attack. The driver commented that the reverse gear selector was not working properly but Smiles saw that the situation had become so desperate that there was nothing for it but to go out through the wire for 500 yards, then swing across the road. The Maxim was then traversed to its limit and raked the lines of advancing infantry, who immediately went to ground and began to fire back. Smiles decided to withdraw a little way towards the Russian lines. The driver selected reverse, let in the clutch and the engine stalled. Smiles jumped over the side and swung the starting handle. The engine fired briefly, then cut out. Once more, Smiles tried to start the engine manually, without success. The car was taking hits continuously. Smiles was hit in the rump and sent sprawling. He rolled into a shallow roadside ditch and was followed by his crew, PO Classey and Leading PO Graham. Both volunteered to try and start the engine but Smiles forbade it. Graham was sent back along the ditch to report to Shadwell, with instructions that no Russian lives were to be lost in attempts to recover the car. Any movement of the crew attracted heavy fire. At length the Bulgarian artillery began to shell the car, without result. Dusk turned to darkness and Classy went out and swung the starting handle. The engine fired but reverse was still unobtainable. The car was bounced across the shallow ditch, turned, then bounced back on to the road, regaining the Russian lines without incident.

On the opposite flank Shadwell had reached the barbed wire and opened up with his Maxim. He immediately attracted heavy return fire and after he received a wound in the neck the car was driven out of action by PO Ash. In the centre the two heavies experienced no difficulty in halting the Bulgarians in spite of their ammunition shortage and, as MacDowell's report shows, they eventually became the specific target of the enemy's artillery.

The enemy infantry were advancing in rushes on the Russian advance post. I opened fire on them at 700 yards with the Maxim and checked the advance slightly, but they started to dig themselves in about 400 yards away. I did not open fire with the Maxim until I observed a group of four or five men. I obtained two boxes of 3-pounder ammunition from Sub-Lieutenant Henderson's car, and later six more boxes of 3-pounder ammunition from which we went out of action to get from Lieutenant Edwards about 11.30 a.m. I continued in action only firing when I observed a target until 5 p.m., when the shellfire at the entrance to the village got so intense that I thought it advisable to take the car out of action.

Balgramo was delighted with the results of the day's fighting. The Russian line to the right and left might have caved in, but, contrary to general expectations, Vizurul had been held, thanks mainly to the British cars. True, the Russians had sustained 290 casualties, but the fact that no less than 380 Bulgarian rifles were picked up that night in front of the trenches suggests that the enemy's loss was much the greater.

On 27 September Smiles took *Ulster* down the Roobla road and treated the Bulgarians to protracted machine-gun fire until his ammunition was exhausted. Try as they might, the enemy's artillery failed to hit him and when they came too close he simply advanced or retired the car a suitable distance. Next day orders were received to withdraw from the potentially dangerous Vizurul salient. After dark the Russian retreat was covered by two Ford armoureds under the command of Lieutenant Hunter and Sub-Lieutenant Kidd. The cars maintained their fire across no man's land for three-quarters of an hour and then joined the Russian rearguard. In so doing, Kidd's vehicle fell into one of the many shell holes, smashing its steering arms beyond repair. After the Maxim had been stripped out, the engine, radiator and petrol tank were destroyed; the party then passed through the marching Russians to the squadron's new headquarters at Locul Sarat.

In the meantime, hard work had restored the rest of the unit's armoured cars to fighting efficiency. Gregory informed General Zurikoff, commanding the Russian Sixth Army, of the fact and the latter requested the formation of a second squadron to cover Sirelius' right flank. Special Service Squadron B was therefore formed for the purpose under Wells-Hood. It consisted of one Rolls Royce and two Lanchester armoured cars, a Pierce Arrow heavy, three Lanchester lorries, an ambulance and a staff car. It departed Tudor Vladimirescu in a blinding snowstorm, but was able to carry out a number of patrols without contacting the enemy and was recalled to Galatz on 4 January.

In the meantime Smiles had been in action at Braila on 1 January, meeting by far the heaviest response from the enemy's artillery that he had encountered thus far. This suggested that the enemy was building up the strength for a final push to complete the occupation of the Dobruja, an impression also received by Gregory as he watched the fighting across the river from the quayside at Galatz. The following day Smiles received a further heavy, *Mountjoy*, a replacement for *Londonderry*, whose main armament traverse mechanism had begun to give such trouble that it had to be withdrawn for the fitters' attention. *Ulster* and two Ford armoureds under Lieutenant Hunter were sent back to cover the withdrawal of the 124th Division from Locul Sarat, while Sub-Lieutenant Kidd was sent across the pontoon bridge with *Mountjoy*, commanded by the newly commissioned Sub-Lieutenant Benson, plus a pair of Ford armoureds to hold a bridgehead on the Macin road while the last Russian troops retreated from the Dobruja into Braila. Both tasks were accomplished without incident. A German armoured car had been reported in the Locul Sarat area but when Hunter searched for it no trace could be found. On 4 January Kidd watched the Cossack rearguard screen clatter across the bridge and then crossed himself, after which the bridge was blown behind him.

Meanwhile, Sixth Army Headquarters had indicated that it had re-established itself at Bolgrad. Gregory was given permission for the unit, less Special Service Squadron A, to evacuate Galatz and establish a new base for itself over the Russian frontier at Tiraspol. The remainder of the fighting vehicles had been formed into Special Service Squadron C under Lieutenant-Commander Belt, and was available for the defence of the town while the evacuation proceeded. The back-loading of vehicles and stores by barge to Reni and thence by rail through Bolgrad to Tiraspol was directed by the adjutant, Lieutenant-Commander Dye, and his assistant, Lieutenant Hanna. For the second time Gregory took the Scottish Women's Hospital under his wing and saw them to safety. For a while he was also made responsible for the royal yacht *Prince Ferdinand of Romania*, for which there was no fuel oil, until relieved of this duty by the Imperial Russian Navy. By the 11th the evacuation was complete and the unit had established itself at Tiraspol.

Chapter 6

Alone in a Sea of Troubles

Locker Lampson reached his unit's new base at Tiraspol on 15 January 1917 in the foulest of moods. He was fully aware that his men knew of his comfortable months spent at home while they were fighting in the mud of the Dobruja. Most would say nothing, of course, although a polite few might enquire whether he had enjoyed his leave, and he clearly had to make up a lot of ground with them. Because of recent events Gregory had become their leader and for him Locker Lampson had developed feelings not merely of jealousy but also of dislike bordering on hatred.

Having decided that Gregory must go, he picked a fight with him, criticising aspects of command techniques. Gregory was regular Royal Navy and he was not going to stand for that from a civilian in uniform who owed his rank to politics and influence, even if he was his superior officer. He rejoined sharply that those same techniques had sufficed for well over half the unit's history. Locker Lampson knew it and could only react by flinging his seniority into the balance. Tempers rose and things were said that led Gregory to decide that it would be in the general interest if the two stayed out of each other's way. He moved onto the Romanian royal family's yacht, the *Prince Ferdinand*, which had already been placed under his protection during the fighting and now, having been refuelled, was being used to supply Smiles at Galatz.

That was not enough for Locker Lampson, who wanted his dagger well and truly thrust home into Gregory's back. In a despatch to the Secretary of the Admiralty he comments

As to Commander Gregory, he really has done very well and deserves his promotion to full Commander. *He does not want a*

DSO and I do not wish to recommend him for one. But he deserves his promotion and I would respectfully ask for this.

Locker Lampson was also averse to his officers being awarded decorations, his reason being that they should not require such incentives to perform their duty. In this respect, however, he was outflanked by the Russians who, following the end of the Dobruja campaign, awarded no fewer than twenty St George's Crosses for distribution to the unit's deserving officers and twenty-six St George's Medals for non-commissioned personnel. Locker Lampson's reaction was cold-eyed to say the least. He wrote to the Admiralty regarding the part played by Lieutenant Smiles during the fighting:

> This officer cannot very well be refused a decoration as the Russians are giving him a St George's Cross and have said something about asking the English Government to decorate him also.

Understandably, their commanding officer's attitudes created something of an atmosphere in the Ward Room, so much so that the unit's senior Russian liaison officer, Captain Baron Girard de Contacon, a former cavalryman who had transferred to his country's armoured car service, was aware of it. He recognised that Locker Lampson was averse to his officers being awarded decorations of higher value than his own and explained the problem to General Sirelius. The latter pointed out that a higher Russian decoration than the St George's Cross could not be awarded for the Dobruja fighting, in which Locker Lampson had played no part. On the other hand, such an award might be backdated to the unit's time in the Caucasus, although one might have expected the Grand Duke Nicholas to have raised the subject himself if it had ever crossed his mind. Shortly after, Sirelius penned a short note to Locker Lampson:

On the occasion of your decoration with the Order of St Vladimir of the 4th Class for the fighting done by your division *under you* in the Caucasus, I take the opportunity of congratulating you upon the Emperor's gracious acknowledgement and I desire to express to you my admiration of the fighting qualities and the conduct of the British armoured cars side by side with the forces of the 4th Siberian Corps.

The outstanding bravery and unqualified gallantry of Lieut Smiles have written a fine page in British military annals and give me the opportunity of requesting for him the decoration of the highest order, namely the St George of the 4th Class.

I beg you to accept the assurances of my complete support,

L. Sirelius,
General.

Outnumbered and outgunned, Locker Lampson had no alternative but to submit his own recommendation that Smiles should be awarded the DSO, albeit reluctantly. However, while he was temporarily absent, Gregory played into his hands by overreacting to a breach of discipline. Locker Lampson promptly wrote to the Admiralty in vindictive terms:

I have the honour to request that a former letter of mine requesting that Commander Gregory should take command of this force in the event of anything happening to me might be ignored, as this officer has recently been ill from the hard work he underwent in the Dobruja.

I would respectfully request that if anything should happen to me, Lieutenant Commander Belt may take over command of this force.

The etiquette of the service required that the letter should be shown to Gregory. It also required that he, having apparently lost his commanding officer's confidence, should request an immediate transfer, which was granted. He left the unit for the United Kingdom shortly after and applied for a return to sea duty. Happily, Locker Lampson's jaundiced views failed to affect Their Lordships' good opinion of Gregory and he was given command of the Flower-class sloop *Mimosa*, which he joined at Malta in November 1917, being engaged in convoy escort duty between Bizerta and Alexandria. In July 1918 he turned over, with his entire ship's company, to *Mimosa*'s sister ship *Veronica*, at Genoa. For the remainder of the war *Veronica* served with the anti-submarine force supporting the Otranto Barrage.

With Gregory out of the way, Locker Lampson was able to turn his attention to other matters. He paid regular visits to the Romanian royal family who, having been forced to abandon their capital, were now resident in their palace at Jassy. A mutual and long-lasting attraction developed between him and Queen Marie, so that he was able to write of his visits, 'I truly became one of the family'. During this period a consignment of steel helmets reached his unit. The Russian Army did not possess steel helmets and he felt that to issue his own men with them would generate ill-feeling. He staged a successful demonstration, placing a helmet on the ground and shooting holes in it with a revolver to demonstrate that the helmets apparently provided little or no protection.

Shortly before these events, Smiles had received promotion to lieutenant commander and his detachment at Galatz continued to make life difficult for the Bulgarians throughout February, March and April. During the period that snow still lay thick upon the ground, armoured cars were painted white and their crews, wearing snow suits, mounted them on railway wagons and pushed them silently along the track up to the enemy lines where they inflicted heavy casualties on the startled Bulgarians. With considerable labour, three 3-pounder guns on field carriages were ferried across the River Sereth and carefully emplaced so that as the morning light grew they methodically destroyed pre-selected targets, including concrete observation posts and machine-gun nests. Russian senior and staff officers thoroughly approved of these forays, but the average Russian infantryman, sick of fighting and wishing only to be left in peace, did not as they invariably attracted a response from the Bulgarian artillery and the result was that the popularity of the British unit declined. With the melting of the snow, however, trenches flooded to a depth of four feet and became uninhabitable. Fraternisation with the enemy, seemingly beyond the control of the Russian officers, became commonplace. Worse still, the number of desertions increased, indicating that the growing mood among the Russians was that they would soldier no more and simply walk home, given half a chance. It was apparent to some of the British officers that a growing number of their allies had reached the limit of their endurance.

Locker Lampson and Girard travelled to St Petersburg in February to negotiate replacements for the vehicles and other equipment that had been lost during the Dobruja fighting. They stayed at the Astoria Hotel and were still there when serious bread riots quickly gathered strength on 8 March. The unrest grew daily and by Sunday 11 March had reached such proportions that the city's Military Governor, General Khabalov, decided to clear the streets. It was a disastrous decision. The police opened fire, killing several score demonstrators, but failed to control the situation. The Cossacks, the traditional bulwark of the monarchy, were sent in but their sympathies lay with the people and some of them even fired on the police. The following day Khabalov sent in the infantry regiments of the Imperial Guard. After three years of war, most of the guardsmen were simply civilians in uniform who were not prepared to fire on their own people with whose cause they sympathised. One by one they mutinied, shooting or confining their least popular officers. Together, soldiers and civilians stormed the police stations then forced the surrender of the fortress of St Peter and St Paul during the afternoon. Khabalov held out in the Admiralty building until the 13th, but by then the Revolution was an accomplished fact. Troops sent by STAVKA to put down the rebellion simply joined it. The Tsar, hurrying to the capital by train, was intercepted at Pskov.

By telephone, he spoke to the Grand Duke Nicholas, General Alexeiev and General Brusilov, each of whom advised him that the chance for constitutional reform was now long past and only his abdication would suffice. He abdicated on behalf of himself and his son the Tsarevich, but transferred the crown to his brother the Grand Duke Michael who, after discussions with leading political figures on 16 March, also abdicated, commenting that he would resume the crown if it were to be offered to him by a constituent assembly. Of course subsequent events prevented any such thing and the long reign of the House of Romanov was at an end.

The final shots of the Revolution had been fired into the crowd by a group of diehards from the roof of the Astoria Hotel. As armed men rushed into the building to deal with them the commotion caused a young and attractive princess to swoon into the conveniently waiting arms of Oliver Locker Lampson, who saw to it that she came to no harm. In other respects, too, the Commander benefited from the upheaval. His negotiations with Alexander Kerensky, War Minister and subsequently Prime Minister of the hurriedly-formed Provisional Government, resulted in his unit being issued with eight Fiat armoured cars, plus petrol tankers, machinery wagons, supply lorries, touring cars, motor cycles and pedal cycles. He also found that his standing with his superiors in London had increased far beyond expectations as his despatches described the Revolution and the steady disintegration of Russian society as power passed into the hands of workers' and soldiers' committees.

At Tiraspol some of the latter demanded that the RACD personnel should send delegates to their meetings. Language difficulties apart, these were overheated shouting affairs in which nothing of value was agreed, creating the opinion that Russian politics were affairs of the absolute in which compromise was impossible. Naturally, the invitation was refused. This was resented by the Russians, some of whom deliberately sabotaged British operations, with the result that two men were killed and four wounded. On 23 April it was rumoured that the British 'warmongers' were to be attacked. The unit stood to all night with the crews manning the Maxims in the cars while the rest of the men were each armed with seventy-five rounds of rifle ammunition. Faced with this, the threat faded away, but on 20 May a vicious brawl took place outside the British billets, one Russian being killed and Petty Officer Bunny Smith being so seriously injured that he died shortly after.

Kerensky had assured Russia's allies that his country would continue to play its part in the war against the Central Powers, assuring them that the Russian Army would mount a major offensive on the Eastern Front during the summer months. British, French and Belgian officers serving in Russia all expressed serious doubts as to whether the Russians were capable of maintaining such an offensive. In private, Kerensky was troubled by similar worries and decided that the major part would be played by non-Russian troops. These included the RNACD, Polish regiments, a Serbian division, Czecho-Slovak battalions recruited from prisoner of war camps, only too keen to fight against their former Austro-Hungarian masters, Belgian machine gunners and French fighter pilots. Guns and ammunition were being concentrated to provide one of the heaviest and most prolonged opening barrages in the history of the Russian artillery. That the offensive was to take place in Galicia had, unfortunately, become something of an open secret.

The RACD left Tiraspol and moved north into Galicia with an attractive landscape consisting of wooded hills and valleys during the early part of June. During the coming offensive the unit would form part of XLI Corps belonging to Seventh Army and its objective would be the heavily fortified town of Brzezany, located within a hollow surrounded by steep hills, and held by three German and two Hungarian regiments. Only two roads, one on either flank, led into the objective and it was planned to employ the cars along these, No. 3 Squadron under Lieutenant Commander Ruston from Doobsche and Nos. 1 and 2 Squadrons under respectively Lieutenant Commander Smiles and Lieutenant Commander Wells Hood from Lietyatin. The general order for all three squadrons was to enfilade the enemy's trenches and stay ahead of the advancing infantry at all times.

At this point the unit found itself saddled with an additional responsibility. The Russian Army had never taken to using trench mortars and the head of the British Mission in St Petersburg, Brigadier General Poole, was anxious to demonstrate the value of such weapons. The problem was that in the country's present disorganised state, actually getting the weapons to the front was fraught with difficulties. Locker Lampson was informed that some sixty tons of 2- and 4-inch mortars and ammunition had been despatched to the unit's railhead, which was fifty miles behind the front, accompanied by a small team of instructors. It took Sub-Lieutenant Lefroy and his supply echelon twenty-four hours' continuous work to bring everything forward and distribute it along the corps frontage. The Russian staff officers were delighted by the arrival of such weapons but in the absence of prior training for their men requested that they should be manned by RACD men. In addition, they requested that certain of the more important machine-gun posts along the front should become a British responsibility as this would bolster the confidence of their own men. The result was that the unit had men fighting with every division in the corps and was stretched to its limits manning cars, trench mortars and machine guns as well as emplacing 3-pounder guns.

The supporting barrage lasted for two days, reaching its climax at 05.17 on 1 July, when the trench mortars joined in its final stages. At 09.55 Wells Hood led out his squadron in the Rolls armoured, gathering speed as the cars tore along the road through bursting shells with a hail of bullets clattering off their armour. It took only minutes to reach the outer line of enemy trenches, which were raked to right and left. Foolishly, the survivors tried to escape across open ground and were immediately cut down. While the infantry closed up, the squadron protected the corps' left flank, then forged ahead until further progress along the road was barred by a sandbag and barbed-wire barricade.

Over on the right flank Ruston's squadron also made considerable progress. In addition to his cars, Ruston had also sited three machine guns and a 3-pounder under Lieutenant Turner to dominate the enemy trenches. These were causing the Germans such trouble that, as the day progressed, they mounted a counter-attack in battalion strength. Ruston allowed them to reach open ground between the lines, then opened up, inflicting heavy losses. The counter-attack sank into the ground but by now the enemy artillery had identified the position of Turner's guns and opened fire on them, using a mixture of high explosive and gas shells. Several men, including Turner, were hit and one received fatal injuries. Elsewhere, one of Sub-Lieutenant de Coninck's two Maxims was knocked out, three of the detachment being killed and the remainder wounded. Despite this, the surviving gun remained in action until mid-afternoon. Simultaneously, Sub-Lieutenant Woods' detachments accounted for a number of enemy machine-gun posts, until subjected to such a rain of gas shells that their masks were unable to cope.

The British had done everything that had been asked of them at the modest cost of five killed and six wounded, but the performance of the Russians had been every bit as mixed as had been feared. Two Trans-Amur regiments actually fought their way through Brzezany Wood and into the outskirts of the town itself but retired to their own lines when their supports refused to advance. Polish troops deserted in large numbers to the Germans opposite, who allowed them to walk home through their lines. In their shame, Russian officers, and even a priest, advanced alone to their deaths, having failed to persuade their men to follow them. Farther south, there were some isolated successes to report as equally disillusioned Austrian formations produced mass surrenders. The Czech 81st Regiment marched across no man's land and then, with band playing and Colours flying, marched through Tarnopol; it subsequently joined the legendary Czech Legion that fought its way home along the Trans-Siberian Railway during the Russian Civil War. In the meantime, some of its members even asked

Locker Lampson to supply them with armoured cars so that they could fight against their former Habsburg masters.

Such things apart, no doubt existed that Kerensky's offensive had failed before it had properly begun. It was also clear that in its present state the Russian Army was barely capable of defensive tasks. By 4 July the Germans had re-occupied their old positions and the lines were exactly as they were before the offensive began. On 8 July the German heavy artillery inflicted a series of direct hits on Russian supply and ammunition dumps in the area of Kozova, eight miles behind the front, in the area of which the RACD had its forward base. Heavy explosions continued throughout the day, littering the ground with shell fragments and cases. Over all a huge pall of smoke rose hundreds of feet into the air, spreading outwards at its summit to resemble the shape of a tree. Locker Lampson was informed that the dumps contained gas shells, that half a million tons of dynamite had yet to explode and that he must move his unit's own ammunition and explosive supplies out of harm's way. With the help of some Russian cars this was accomplished in four hours. For the Russians, however, the loss of several months' ammunition supply, including heavy calibre rounds that could only be obtained from England, was an unmitigated disaster. Without the slightest justification the Cossacks blamed the Jewish community, killing several of its members out of hand.

On 18 July General Lavr Kornilov replaced Brusilov as Commander-in-Chief and two days later Kerensky took over from Prince Lvov as Prime Minister. At this period any measures passed by the Provisional Government had to be approved by the St Petersburg Soviet Workers' and Soldiers' Soviet, over which the arch-revolutionary Lenin and his Bolshevik comrades were steadily tightening their grip. Obviously, this situation was far from ideal, although the fact that the Soviet had the support of the St Petersburg garrison meant that it had to be tolerated. Lenin despised democracy as a form of government and was impatient to impose his own version of centralised autocratic power. During the period known to Communist historians as The July Days, he attempted to stage a coup but he was less popular than he imagined and was thwarted by disinterested elements of the garrison. He was forced into hiding and some of his supporters, notably Leon Trotsky, were briefly imprisoned. Despite this, his determination to secure absolute power for himself remained unshaken.

During this period senior German and Austrian officers were analysing the results of Kerensky's offensive and the only possible conclusion they could draw was that the Russian Army was on the verge of disintegration. On 16 July nine Central Powers divisions attacked the Russian Eleventh Army on the Tarnopol sector and within days the front had been ruptured, apparently beyond repair. During the evening of 20 July Locker Lampson received a signal from XLI Corps to the effect that his unit was now under the command of Eleventh Army, on whose left flank it would be working. Within two hours all the cars, their fuel, ammunition and food having been replenished, had reached Kozova at daybreak. The only hard information that staff officers could supply was that the enemy had penetrated to a depth of twenty-five miles and that, for the moment, the RACD was given carte blanche to deal with the situation as it thought fit.

For the next ten days the small British unit fought for its life in conditions that made its earlier battles in the Dobruja seem highly organised. At first, the Austrians were as exhausted as the Russians and had outrun their artillery. The cars, therefore, experienced no difficulty in holding their own and inflicting heavy losses on the Austrian infantry. However, as the enemy's artillery came into the line the situation became progressively more difficult. The heavy *Ulster* broke down and attempts to repair it had to be abandoned when the Austrians were only fifty yards distant, although the working parts of the guns were removed to prevent their use. With a prolonged cheer the Austrians swarmed out of their trenches and advanced on the Russian positions at a trot. The Russians bolted and fled, abandoning their machine guns, flinging aside their rifles and removing their boots so that they could run the faster. Gripped by hysteria and sheer animal fear, they piled aboard some of the armoured cars, demanding to be driven to safety, until their combined weight proved too much for the engines of the larger cars, which stalled, or for the suspensions of the little Ford armoureds. One car, at least, is believed to have fired over the Russians' heads to prevent being swamped.

And so it continued, day after day. If the crews were not fighting they were repairing their cars, restoring them to fighting trim or moving from one threatened sector to another with little time or no time for food, sleep or rest. A yawning gap in the Russian line had been covered by skilful deployment and repeatedly halted the Austro-German advance, so buying priceless time for the harassed Russian command. Prisoners stated that the cars seemed to be present whichever way they advanced, and that there was a general belief that the unit was three or four times its actual size. Further interrogations suggested that some 600 casualties had been inflicted during the fighting at Darakoov, and probably not less than 2,000 for the entire retreat. There was no doubt that the Germans regarded the British as the only serious opposition. The entire range of armoured car tactics had been employed and although communications had been restricted to hand signals and messages passed by despatch rider, tactical control had never broken down.

As the Russian collapse had not been confined to the Galician front, the Provisional Government and even the St Petersburg Soviet, terrified by the monster they had created between them, readily agreed to Kornilov's demand that the officers' authority, together with the death penalty, must be restored. Long railway trains, flanked by Cossack battle police, were drawn up across level crossings, ruthlessly exposing those with phoney wounds and marching them back into the line under escort while others, apparently unharmed, received summary justice. Such measures were necessary, for there were no fewer than 40,000 armed and dangerous deserters present in Gusiatyn alone. That particular problem was solved by the arrival of the aptly named Wild Division, recruited from semi–savage and barely disciplined Caucasian

Muslim Cossacks, who disliked the Revolution because it threatened to sweep away the privileges conferred on them by the Tsar. Locker Lampson strictly forbade his men to become involved in the restoration of Russian discipline, but he supplied the Wild Division with a dozen Lewis guns and 50,000 rounds of ammunition. Overjoyed, they spent the night galloping through the streets of the town, blazing away from the saddle, after which the crowds of undesirables were less in evidence. There was no doubt that the Wild Division meant business, but its methods disgusted those of the British unit who saw them at work. A group of political activists holding a meeting were shot down. A party of deserters was threatened with decimation unless they revealed the identity of the agitator who had led them away from the front. This they did and when the man confessed he was shot dead and his body nailed to a tree with a warning notice in Russian and German. A Guards' regiment that had murdered its commanding officer and battalion commanders was forced to surrender after a pitched battle and similarly dealt with.

Following these episodes the RACD were called forward twice during the next week but were not committed to action. It was Locker Lampson's view that if the Austro-German offensive was renewed the front would almost certainly disintegrate. He set about back-loading hundreds of tons of stores from Proskurov to the unit's rear base at Kursk and established a fresh base at Brovari, near Kiev. He also felt that civil war had become a distinct possibility and despatched those of his wounded who could be moved direct to England by way of Kiev and Archangel.

At the end of August Russia lurched a step closer towards internal strife. Kornilov was keen to curb the unwarranted interference of the St Petersburg garrison not only in political matters, but also in the running of the railways and industrial relations, particularly as its members were pointedly disinterested in performing active service and remained snug in their barracks. Kerensky could have made a valuable ally of him had he not disliked his right-wing views. Instead, when

Kornilov, tired of waiting for the Provisional Government to act, let it be known that he intended marching on the capital, using the Wild Division as his advance guard, Kerensky initially assured him that his demands were acceptable then, after the Germans had captured the Baltic city of Riga on 3 September, denounced him as a traitor. Once more, thousands poured out onto the streets of St Petersburg, arms being handed to anyone who wanted them by the Soviet, who also supplied the Bolsheviks who assured them that they would never fight for Kerensky but gladly fight against Kornilov. The latter began his march on 8 September and ended the following day when the Wild Division declared itself unwilling to fight against the government. Kornilov was arrested but managed to escape some months later and was killed during the civil war. Simultaneously, Kerensky assumed the mantle of Commander-in-Chief which sat uneasily on his shoulders as the Bolsheviks flatly refused to hand in their weapons.

Meanwhile, throughout August and September, Locker Lampson back-loaded his unit's cars, stores and equipment to Kursk, its winter quarters. The open hostility now exhibited by the Russian population convinced him that he must get as many of his men as possible out of Russia, using 'overdue' home leave as an excuse, leaving only a small care and maintenance party behind during the winter months. The first party, forty-eight strong, left for Archangel on 22 August, and the main body followed a fortnight later. Moscow was in a state of uproar following the Kornilov affair and the British personnel were confined to the station for their own safety. On one of the northbound trains the surly engine crew had to be bribed with tobacco and bully beef every few miles and eventually refused to go any further. Unfortunately for them, two petty officers were experienced railwaymen who took over the engine and brought the train safely into Archangel. In the circumstances it seems highly unlikely that Russian crews were permitted to retain their *pourboire*. Russia's wealthy and middle class citizens, together with those holding moderate opinions and others who felt they no longer had a place in their country had already begun to leave in large numbers and were only too happy to pay in cash or kind for a passage or assistance in finding one. As a result, some of the unit's personnel left Russia a lot better off than they entered it, their consciences eased by the knowledge that they had acted in a humanitarian cause. Some of the RNACD men embarked on their old friend the *Umona*, others aboard the Russian liner *Dvinsk*, and the majority aboard the *Stentor*, described as a 'very decent boat' which fed them well. The voyage home was uneventful and they landed at various East Coast ports at the end of October. As yet, the Admiralty had not decided what to do with the unit and they were sent on extended block leave.

Back at Kursk the rear party, under Commander Soames, lived out a lonely existence in the midst of an indifferent population. The Bolshevik coup which destroyed the Provisional Government took place during the night of 6/7 November. Far from being the epic struggle of Communist myth, it acquired its objectives with such ridiculous ease that most of St Petersburg was unaware that anything had happened until proclamations were made the following day to the effect that the Soviet was now the supreme authority. During elections for a Constituent Assembly the Bolsheviks polled less than one quarter of the vote. The answer of Lenin and his bully boys was to make the Assembly unworkable and then disband it. Civil War therefore became inevitable.

The British rear party at Kursk was left to its own devices until first light on Christmas Day when armed men disarmed the sentry on the gate. The officers' quarters were then surrounded and Soames was ordered to hand over the unit's cars, guns and military stores. It was soon apparent to Soames that he was dealing with rather junior Bolsheviks whom he informed that he was only prepared to discuss such matters with the Commissar himself. He then telephoned Admiral Stanley, his immediate superior, in St Petersburg. The admiral told him to concede as little as possible and to avoid bloodshed at all costs.

The Commissar reached the base to find that everyone was now up and in a very nasty mood. He quickly learned that in the British service the relationship between officers and men was very different to that in the Russian armed services and was told in no uncertain manner that holding British officers at gunpoint was bitterly resented, as was the fact that the Bolsheviks had chosen Christmas Day to invade the British camp – the Russian Christmas does not take place until 7 January in the western calendar – and had obviously been planned to take place while the British were celebrating. Furthermore, Soames continued, the Maxim machine guns were in the men's billets, as were their personal weapons and an adequate supply of ammunition for both. With difficulty, he prevented an attack on some Bolsheviks who had penetrated the vehicle park. Rattled, the Commissar pretended that no less than 5,000 Red Guards were surrounding the camp and would storm it if his demands were not met. Detecting a nervous quiver in the Commissar's tone, Soames replied that he was welcome to the cars, which were useless and only at the base for repairs, but he was keeping the unit's transport vehicles for its own use. Meanwhile, Christmas had a special significance for the British and he suggested that if the Commissar and his comrades wished to avoid a bloodbath they should leave the barracks at once. To save face, the Commissar left a pair of sentries at the gate. The British then set to, rendering the cars and guns useless by removing or smashing vital moving parts.

It seemed that no arrangements had been made by the Commissar for the feeding of his sentries, so they were given food at the British kitchen at certain times. They also attended the unit's Christmas and New Year concert parties and generally enjoyed themselves so much that they punctiliously saluted the British officers and even requested permission to join the RACD. The one thing they did not do was prevent members of the unit from going into town (against Soames' advice) with the result that some of the men spent Christmas with Russian families.

On 8 January a group from the Moscow Soviet appeared, demanding armoured cars and weapons. Soames suggested that they consult their Kursk comrades. Whatever was said between the two parties quickly

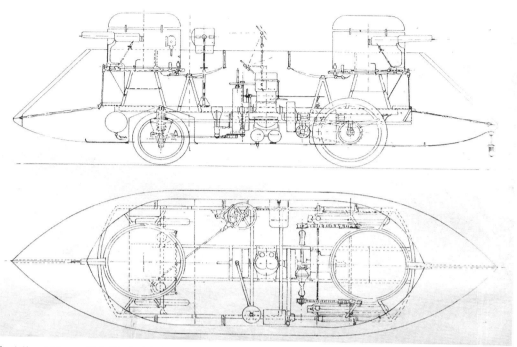

1. (*Above*) Plans of Mr Frederick Sims' 'War Car' that appeared in the April 1902 edition of *The Autocar*. The War Office was not impressed, commenting that 'However private gentlemen chose to spend their time was entirely their own business'. The car was vulnerable to any form of fire from above and the life expectancy of the commander's periscope could be measured in minutes.

2. (*Right*) Mr Sims, seen here manning a machine gun, was not, however, a man to give up easily. He managed to sell at least one of a smaller version of his car to an East African railway company which was tired of having its permanent way plundered by others who found alternative uses for the metal. These vehicles were fitted with flanged wheels permitting them to operate along the track.

3. (*Left*) When war broke out in 1914 it was the Royal Naval Air Service that convinced the Admiralty and, later, the War Office, that a use existed for armoured vehicles fitted with weapons. Many patriotic citizens, including a sizeable number of Rolls Royce owners, donated their vehicles for use in this way. The illustration shows an armoured Rolls Royce fitted with a machine-gun turret. Its Petty Officer crew are still wearing their blue temperate climate landing rig.

4. (*Right*) Active service revealed that the smaller cars sometimes required the assistance of a more heavily armed vehicle. These began entering service in 1915. Pictured here is a Seabrook heavy armoured car armed with a 3-pdr gun mounted on a turntable. If necessary, part of the side armour could be lowered, as shown. The gun could be dismounted for towing on a specially constructed carriage.

5. (*Left*) Another heavy armoured car which entered service in 1915 was the Pierce-Arrow, the 3-pdr gun of which was mounted in a traversing turret. On balance, the 'heavies' gave a good account of themselves, but their weight was a handicap in soft going. In theory, each armoured car section included one 'heavy'.

6. (*Above*) The RNACD section of Rolls Royce armoured cars committed to the fighting on the Gallipoli peninsula saw only limited action because the front resembled that on the Western Front, where movement was prevented by trench lines and barbed-wire entanglements. The cars spent most of their time in these dugouts, which offered some defence against the Turkish artillery, and took part in the general evacuation.

7. (*Left*) Hugh Grosvenor, 2nd Duke of Westminster, seen here in the uniform of the Royal Horse Guards (The Blues) raised an armoured car unit from among his friends and estate staff. The unit was despatched to Egypt when the Senussi invasion from neighbouring Libya threatened the political stability of the area.

8. (*Left*) A section of the Duke's units at one of its Egyptian bases. The young officer in the foreground, together with his driver and fitter, are being photographed for 'the folks at home'.

9. (*Right*) The Duke's cars routing the Senussi at Agagyia, just one of the battles at which they earned their glamorous reputation. The artist was not familiar with Rolls Royce armoured cars, but his picture describes what happened accurately enough.

10. (*Above*) Once the threat posed by the Senussi had been dealt with, the Duke's unit returned to the UK and the security of the Western Desert became the responsibility of Light Car Patrols. These consisted of Model T Fords armed with Lewis guns, and motor cyclists. They produced the desert maps used in the Second World War and introduced many elements of desert safety including the priority of radiators for any water supply, air recognition panels, maintaining stated routes and adequate supplies of rations, vehicle spares and tyres.

11. (*Right*) Commander Oliver Locker Lampson MP RNVR commanded the most widely travelled armoured car unit of the First World War. Undoubtedly liked by his men, he employed unbelievably devious methods to obtain whatever he wanted but ruthlessly destroyed the career of an officer whose record threatened to outshine his own.

12. (*Left*) Part of Locker Lampson's unit, which consisted mainly of Lanchester armoured cars, attracting attention of local children as it passed through Trans-Caucasia on the first of its campaigns.

12a. (*Below*) A model T Ford light armoured car used by Locker Lampson's unit.

13. (*Below*) The Australian Armoured Car Section was an early arrival in Egypt. It consisted of (centre) a chain-driven Mercedes, which was later deprived of its turret; right, a Daimler mounting, first, a Renault 37mm cannon and, then, a Colt machine gun with gunshield, and (left) a Minerva tender.
The section also possessed a motor-cycle combination armed with a Colt machine gun. The cars were returned to Australia in 1917. Some of the section transferred to the British 11th and 12th LAMBs (Light Armoured Motor Batteries), while others formed the 7th (Australian) Light Car Patrol.

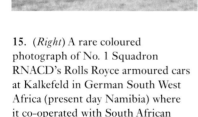

14. (*Left*) The 7th (Australian) Light Car Patrol photographed shortly after its formation. The unit greatly distinguished itself, notably during the First Battle of Gaza.

15. (*Right*) A rare coloured photograph of No. 1 Squadron RNACD's Rolls Royce armoured cars at Kalkefeld in German South West Africa (present day Namibia) where it co-operated with South African troops.

The RNAS Rolls-Royce Armoured Cars
of the 1st. Squadron of the RNACD
in German South West Africa, ca. June 1915.

16. (*Left*) Following the German surrender in South West Africa, most of No. 1 Squadron returned to the UK but four of its cars were shipped round the Cape and served in German East Africa, known then as Tanga and now as Tanzania. In this theatre the unit became known as No. 10 (RN) Armoured Motor Battery.

17. (*Left*) Campfire scene in East Africa. The Rolls Royce crew allow two *askaris* to examine what must have seemed a very strange machine indeed.

8. (*Right*) Also serving in East Africa as an armoured car unit raised privately by Sir John Willoughby, a participant in the Jameson Raid. Sir John insisted that his four-car battery should be known as No. 1 (Willoughby's) Armoured Motor Battery – the crew's neck protector cloths, not seen since the Battle of Omdurman, provide a nice 'private army' touch. The Leylands were well designed in many ways but were too heavy for what was asked of them in East Africa, witness the deep rutting caused by the wheels despite their being fitted with wide flanges.

19. (*Left*) The 4.1-in guns salvaged from the German cruiser SMS *Konigsberg*, sunk in the Rufifi river by the monitors HMS *Severn* and *Mersey*, would have provided the British armoured car crews with a headache had they been employed against them.

0. (*Right*) The Government of India was responsible for the conduct of the war in Mesopotamia. It despatched two Fiat armoured cars to General Townshend, who was conducting an ill-conceived advance on Baghdad. One is seen here being unloaded from a barge on the Euphrates. Both cars fought at the Battle of Ctesiphon, which resulted in a British victory although the heavy casualties sustained forced Townshend to withdraw.

21. (*Left*) Both cars survived the retreat and were not involved in Townshend's disastrous surrender at Kut-al-Amara. Fitted with flanged wheels they were used to patrol the railway line that brought supplies from Basra to the Front and eventually reached Baghdad when the Turkish front was broken. The car in the illustration has been fitted with extra shade against the sun and has two chuggles (canvas bags fill with water) slung behind the cab. Evaporation kept the water cool.

22. (*Right*) When the Turkish army's front was broken in 1917 its retreat quickly became a rout. The scene was sketched as it developed by Private Bagot of the 14th Hussars. On the left the gunboats *Tarantula*, *Mantis* and *Moth* are pursuing a Turkish gunboat; in the middle distance the guns of S Battery RHA are in action and a section of Rolls Royce armoured cars, almost certainly belonging to 6th LAMB, is about to pass through a ruined village; in the foreground a motor cycle despatch rider is arriving with fresh orders for the hussars.

23. (*Left*) In Palestine the Turkish army was destroyed in September 1918 at the Battle of Megiddo. Following the British breakthrough, a Rolls Royce armoured car of 11th or 12th LAMB halts beside the horse lines of a cavalry regiment.

24. (*Right*) The pursuit lasted for 350 miles and, due to the horses' exhaustion, its final stages were carried out by mechanised units. The photograph shows 12th LAMB and 7th (Australian) Light Car Patrol halted at the roadside near outside Aleppo.

Major General S.C. Dunsterville

25. (*Left*) Major General Lionel Dunsterville was given the apparently impossible task of denying the Turks the benefits of the Baku oilfield in Trans-Caucasian Russia, itself now torn by civil war. Somehow he succeeded.

26. (*Below*) Duncars' route entailed crossing the mountain ranges separating Mesopotamia from Persia, negotiating the Persian hinterland to the port of Enzeli and as shown crossing the Caspian Sea to Baku itself. The difficulties were enormous and it took a unit as experienced as this to overcome them.

27. (*Left*) A poor but very interesting photo demonstrating the difficulties of changing the incredibly heavy Rubberine tyres. Digging a hole under the vehicle provided a better solution than a conventional jack.

28. (*Below*) The efficiency of an armoured unit is only as good as its technical back-up. Duncars' chain-drive Republic machinery wagon has narrowly escaped tumbling over the edge of the dreadful Enzeli road.

29. (*Left*) Another of Dunsterville's problems was supply. It had taken this convoy of Model T Fords a week to cover the road from the unit's main base at Baghdad to Enzeli, crossing mountain ranges like that in the background while the summits of other passes were covered in snow and the blistering heat of the plains was replaced by freezing high altitude cold.

30. (*Left*) A local warlord named Mirza Kuchik Khan also tried to get in Dunsterville' way but was finally persuaded to return to civil life by a charge of kukri-wielding Gurkhas led by an Austin armoured car that dispersed his followers. He promised to b good and was allowed to keep his expensive automatic for his own defence.

31. (*Left*) Another poor but interesting photograph showing one of Duncars' Austin in an area of the Baku oilfields known as The Mud Volcano, where some of the heaviest fighting took place.

32. (*Right*) Lieutenant Colonel E. J. Carter, commanding the 17th Battalion Tank Corps, beside one of the battalion's Austin armoured cars, which were armed with Hotchkiss machine guns. The upper part of the vehicle is painted sky blue to aid concealment on crests.

33. (*Left*) To counter unrest in variou parts of the sub-continent, often fomented by German sympathisers, the Indian Government produced a hybrid armoured car/personnel carrier, simply known as the Indian Pattern armoured car. This prototype patriotically named *The King-Emperor* is providing senior officers with a sample ride.

34. (*Right*) The Indian Pattern armoured cars were constructed by railway workshops throughout the country. The builders stuck to the basic plan but introduced local variations in design. Some were fitted with a frontal girder like a submarine's net cutter; this was intended to cut cables or ropes that had been stretched across the road to decapitate crewmen.

degenerated into street fighting as the comrades set about each other. The Kursk faction had managed to assemble one car by cannibalising the others and this could be heard making its contribution to the fracas. Eventually, some sort of drunken reconciliation was cobbled together and both sides arrived at the camp the following day. They blamed the British, first, for starting the fight and, second, for letting the cars get into such a terrible state. Soames assured them that the sole reason for British squadron's presence in Russia was to fight Germans, who had been responsible for damaging the cars in the first place, and that as regards local fighting between Russian political parties its intention was to maintain a policy of strict neutrality, at which the Russians shook hands with each other and everyone else, and dispersed.

With the loss of the armoured cars there was no longer any need for the squadron to remain in Russia. Admiral Stanley informed Soames that a special train was being provided to convey it to Murmansk along the recently completed rail link from St Petersburg and that he should have his men ready to leave Kursk on 12 January. Also aboard would be officials from the Kursk Soviet, almost certainly under orders from St Petersburg to deal with any political difficulties that might be encountered along the way. The train left on time and without further incident but such was the chaos engulfing the Russian railway system that it did not reach Murmansk until 25 January.

Lenin had opened peace negotiations with the Central Powers at Brest Litovsk. He might have thrown his weight about to some effect in the St Petersburg Soviet, but as far as Germany and Austria-Hungary were concerned he had served his purpose and was of no further use to them. Ultimately, he was forced to sign away one-third of Russia's population, the same proportion of the country's crop-yielding farmland, one-quarter of her entire territory, and 27 per cent of her income. For the moment, he signalled Trotsky to the effect that British and Romanian service personnel remaining in Russia were to be arrested. Trotsky, however, was playing a game of his own and, wishing to retain Allied goodwill for as long as possible, despatched his own signal to Murmansk too late for the local Soviet to act on it – not that they would have wished to, as they lived within point-blank range of the four 12-inch guns of the pre-Dreadnought battleship HMS *Glory* which were quite capable of turning the town into a pile of blazing matchwood in short order. Nevertheless, once the British port authorities were aware of the danger, they acted immediately. On 29 January, sixty-one men, including members of the armoured car squadron, military supply and port staff, sailed for the United Kingdom aboard the armed merchant cruiser HMS *Titonus*. The remainder, fifty-six British and twenty-eight Romanians, were taken off the train on 31 January and transferred to HMS *Glory*, where they felt safe for the first time in many months. On 1 February forty ratings of the armoured car squadron, fifteen Romanian officers and thirteen Romanian NCOs, transferred to eight minesweeping trawlers that would take them to Lerwick. They left Murmansk in calm weather, looking rather like ducks on a mill pond, but quickly ran into foul weather in which their passengers suffered the agonies of sea-sickness for days. One trawler, the *Idena*, sprang a leak and sank on 5 February although her passengers and crew were picked up the following day. By the time Lerwick was reached on 9 February, the RACD men had acquired a very high regard for the trawlermen.

As they dispersed to their homes on leave they had many a tale to tell and perhaps a twinge or two of regret that the Great Adventure was over. In fact, it had a further act to be played.

Chapter 7

Around the Dark Continent

Kaiser Wilhelm II was not satisfied with ruling the most militarily efficient empire on the continent of Europe. It was a matter of considerable annoyance to him that France, Holland, Portugal and even little Belgium should have acquired considerable territories in the world's tropical areas, and a particularly irritating fact of life was that his detested cousin, King Edward VII of Great Britain, was capable of reminding him that the British Empire was one on which the sun never set, capable of almost effortless expansion and guarded by the greatest navy in history. Almost choking with rage, Wilhelm claimed that Germany, too, was entitled to acquire her rightful 'place in the sun'. There were, however, several problems involved in turning these words into deeds. First, taken as a whole, only a small percentage of Germans were interested in a colonial lifestyle, the beginnings of which would probably involve years of hardship and possibly danger before their rewards materialised. Second, Germany was a late starter in the scramble for territories so that all that remained for her were areas in which other powers had no interest. They included the treaty port of Tsing Tao in China, several groups of Pacific islands and, in Africa, Togoland, Cameroon, South West Africa (known today as Namibia) and German East Africa (Tanga), the last being subsequently known as Tanganyika and then Tanzania.

The Germans could be harsh colonial masters, demanding serf-like obedience from their native subjects as well as inflicting horrific punishments on those who chose to offer resistance. In South West Africa this pointlessly cruel style of government drove the Herero and Namaqua tribesmen into armed rebellion. Having defeated them in the field the German commander, Lieutenant General Lothar von Trotha, embarked on a policy of genocide, driving the tribes into the Omaheke Desert where the few wells had been deliberately poisoned. As a direct result, it is estimated that approximately 65,000 Herero and 10,000 Namaqua perished in the twentieth century's first deliberate genocide.

In Tanga a similar rebellion, known as the Maji Maji War, took place between the years 1905 and 1907, despite the colony having been more thoroughly developed than was the case in South West Africa. This was an altogether more serious affair that not even the rapid despatch of reinforcements from Germany itself and the German colony of New Guinea could bring under control. Nevertheless, the Governor, Count Gustav von Gotzen, was shocked by the carnage that his troops were inflicting on the rebels and their supporters and offered a full pardon to those who abandoned their leaders and witch doctors and handed in their weapons. This produced the groundwork upon which the next Governor, Dr Heinrich Schnee, was able to introduce a series of social and economic reforms that actually benefited the African population, who now felt that they had something worth fighting for. The outbreak of war in 1914 saw the rapid capture and occupation of Germany's Pacific Ocean colonies by Australian, New Zealand and Japanese troops. In Africa, some German colonies held out much longer than others. For example, Togoland was overrun in 1914, but the German forces in Tanga held out for two weeks after the 1918 Armistice in Europe.

South West Africa was an obvious target for occupation by British and Imperial troops, but invading it involved a number of serious considerations. It occupied no less than 300,000 square miles but at the time it possessed few roads worthy of the name. The only way to get about the interior of the country was by means of its narrow-gauge railway system. From Walfisch Bay and Swakopmund on the coast the line ran inland for almost 200 miles with a branch line heading north-east to Tsumab and Grossfontein. The main line, however, swung south to Windhoek, the capital, where it made an end-on connection with a

line running south for 300 miles before turning west and heading for
Luderitz Bay on the coast. On the way, it was joined at Seeheim on the
Great Fish River by a line running in from Cape Colony. Apart from
this, and the branch line to the north, the system's main line formed a
huge but elongated loop.

When war between the British Empire on the one hand and the
Transvaal and Orange Free State on the other ended in 1902, the
United Kingdom pursued a sensible policy of reconciliation and
reconstruction in the former Boer republics, part of which allowed
farmers to purchase horses at a modest price to replace those lost during
the war. Consequently, a majority of Boers accepted the fact that they
would be better off as citizens of the new self-governing Union of South
Africa than they would have been if the old independent republics
were still in being. However, twelve years is a comparatively short
period where politics are concerned and there were those who bitterly
regretted the passing of the old ways and refused to identify with the
new. Such men formed a Nationalist Party under the leadership of
a former Boer Commando leader, General Christiaan de Wet. Thus,
when the government of the Union, led by two former Boer leaders,
Generals Louis Botha and Jan Smuts, announced that an expedition
was to be mounted against German South West Africa, de Wet felt that
his moment had come and raised the Orange Free State's Nationalists
and their sympathisers in open revolt.

The Boers hold a unique place among the world's fighting men.
They wore no uniform, lived in the saddle, were crack shots, fine
trackers and capable of using terrain to its fullest advantage. Above all,
they recognised the value of mobility and the advantage it conferred
over those who lacked it. In short, they were the ideal irregulars with
an instinctive gift for guerrilla warfare. Unless one had the ability to
deploy overwhelming strength against them, the only effective way to
defeat a Boer force was with another Boer force of comparable size.

De Wet had managed to assemble 5,000 men in an area known as
Mushroom Valley. Botha had taken the field at the head of 6,000 men

drawn from loyal commandos and had wisely avoided involving British or Imperial regular troops. For political reasons, de Wet decided to make a stand in the valley. It was a bad decision as he lost the ensuing battle and his army was dispersed, although for as long as they were able its fragments continued to mount raids. Botha then ordered another veteran, Colonel Coen Brits, to pursue de Wet's main body and force its surrender. Brits immediately broke with tradition, recognising that a mounted pursuit would be unlikely to overtake the rebels whereas by commandeering every passenger vehicle in the area he could employ their speed and mechanical stamina to good effect. There were times when his motor detachment was held up by deep sand and had to dig itself out, and others when vehicles were forced to leave the column and change tyres that had been sliced open by flints, but all the signs were that the gap between pursuers and the pursued was closing steadily. There was evidence, too, that de Wet was aware of the fact and was making for neutral territory. Unable to rest his men and horses or find an unguarded crossing, he was finally run to earth and admitted defeat. Apart from a few isolated incidents, the rebellion was over. That provided grounds for satisfaction, but it was tinged with sadness, for so much of the Boers' history was concerned with the heroic tales of men and their horses, and now those days had been ended forever by machines that smelled and spoke a language of their own but somehow lacked a soul.

It was virtually impossible for the Germans to defend their coastline. Their only naval presence was a small gunboat, the *Eber*, which had been a frequent visitor to Cape Town in time of peace, almost certainly with the object of relieving the endless boredom of her own station. With the coming of war she had vanished over the western horizon into the mid-Atlantic where she transferred her guns to the ocean liner *Cap Trafalgar* which thus became a commerce raider, before continuing her voyage to neutral Brazil and internment. As for *Cap Trafalgar*, she was sunk in a legendary duel with a British commerce raider, the former liner *Carmania*, the course of which is described by the author in his book *The Hunters and the Hunted*.

By early January 1915 both Walfisch Bay and Luderitz Bay (the latter also known by the name Agua Pequena) were firmly in South African hands and it became possible to initiate a combined advance into the enemy's interior. The campaign was planned by General Louis Botha, who also commanded the northern arm of the advance personally. In essence this required an advance from Walfisch Bay directly along the railway to Windhoek. The southern arm, under Lieutenant General Jan Smuts, was divided into three columns. The first, under Colonel Sir Duncan Mackenzie, was to follow the railway eastwards from Luderitz Bay. The second, commanded by Lieutenant General Sir Louis van Deventer, was to advance along the Cape Colony railway to Keetmanshoop on the German system. The third, under Colonel C. A. L. Burrage, would start from Kimberley, then cross Bechuanaland and invade the enemy colony from the east. In the overall context the three columns were to concentrate at Keetmanshoop and then advance northwards to join forces with Botha.

Serving with the latter were the Rolls Royce armoured cars of No. 1 Squadron RNACD. The cars had been landed at Walfisch Bay in April 1915; the comment of its commanding officer, Lieutenant Commander Whittall, was that if it had been possible to carry out a preliminary advance of the route the cars had been ordered to follow they would not have been landed at all. Indeed, so heavy was the going along this that at one point they were each consuming four gallons of petrol and one of water for every mile covered. The only contact between the cars and the enemy had resulted from an early morning reconnaissance flight carried out by the Germans' only aircraft. The squadron's first two cars had reached Trekopjes (Three Hills) by rail when, as usual, the aircraft droned into sight. It carried out its daily examination of the cars and then, to everyone's surprise, dropped two or three 4-inch artillery shells, stabilised for flight, in lieu of conventional bombs. They blew craters in the desert but hit nothing of importance and, disappointed, the pilot turned for home. He promptly reported to the German commander-in-chief, General von Heydebreck, that he had attacked a South African encampment in the sidings of which were two water tankers. This was not an unreasonable conclusion as the cars' circular turrets might indeed suggest such vehicles. Furthermore, their presence would be a logical requirement for any South African advance as the only alternative supply of fresh water was at Nonidas, forty miles closer to the coast. The general, a capable commander who had achieved a minor victory over a force consisting of South African Mounted Rifles and Transvaal Horse Artillery at Sandfontein the previous September, concurred and decided to mount a spoiling attack.

Two days later a South African mounted reconnaissance reported the advance of a German force consisting of two artillery batteries and an infantry brigade. Three more armoured cars had reached Trekopjes but the absence of ramps prevented Whittall's crews from driving them off the railway flats, as did the fact that this section of the line had been constructed on steep-sided embankments. Unexpectedly, this turned out to be an advantage, as the reconnaissance patrol confirmed that the enemy would have to cross the embankment to press home their attack. Whittall therefore ordered the cars to drive along the track itself and engage the enemy as soon as they were within range.

The sleepers made the ride a bumpy one, but as soon as the Germans were within range the cars opened up with their machine guns. The enemy artillery unlimbered and engaged the cars with shrapnel that rattled off the plating in an alarming manner but caused no damage. The German infantry then swarmed to the attack over the embankment but were cut down as the cars traversed their turrets to scythe through their ranks. The attack melted away and the German guns opened fire once more. As they seemed to be getting the range, Whittall ordered the cars to pull back a little way to spoil the enemy's range and then beat off a second infantry attack which once more came to close quarters before failing. A third attack started but quickly melted away and it was clear that the enemy had lost heart. Covered by the fire of their guns, the Germans withdrew. If the cars had been able to carry out a pursuit, as Whittall intended, the effect on the enemy's troops would have been disastrous. Unfortunately, while a place was found at which the cars could descend the embankment, deep sand restricted their speed to a crawl. One of them had sustained a punctured radiator in the engagement and the only casualty among their crews was one man wounded.

The column commander's report emphasised that the cars had played the major role in defeating the enemy's counter counter-attack, and in Windhoek the German press was in complete agreement, commenting on the 'unfairness' of the enemy's use of 'armoured motor cars' which their troops lacked the power to destroy. Heydebreck's African *askaris* attributed something akin to magical powers to them and stayed out of their way whenever possible, although they were not to be seriously employed again during the campaign.

The German commander, informed that all the South African columns were making steady progress, was fully aware that if he was compelled to fight a major action he would be so decisively outnumbered that defeat was a certainty. He accepted that the only course of action remaining to him was to tie down as many of his opponents as possible to prevent their being employed elsewhere. Windhoek could not be defended and was entered on 12 May. By then von Heydebreck was withdrawing into the north-east of the country. A few small engagements took place resulting in the capture of a considerable number of German prisoners, which in itself confirmed that the campaign was drawing to its inevitable conclusion. The last of these actions took place on 2 July at Otavifonetein on the railway's north-eastern branch line. Two days later the Germans, numbering 204 officers and 3,293 other ranks with thirty-seven field guns and twenty-two machine guns, finally surrendered. This was the first military success of a united South African nation fighting under its own senior officers.

Most of the cars were returned to England where they came under the Army's control. However, under the command of Lieutenant

Nalder, four were shipped round the Cape to East Africa, where they were re-designated as the 10th (Royal Navy) Armoured Motor Battery. Their arrival can only have been welcomed as the campaign against the German colony of Tanga had got off to a very bad start indeed.

On 2 November 1914 a British attempt was made to capture the town of Tanga, in the north of the colony, by means of an amphibious landing. The troops involved were known as Force B and were drawn from the Indian Army's 27 Bangalore Brigade and an Imperial Service Brigade. With the exception of two units, the 2nd Loyal (North Lancashire) Regiment and a battalion of the Kashmir Rifles, Force B was completely inexperienced, half-trained and imperfectly disciplined, so was completely unsuited to a venture that required high professional standards. Even so, the formation was 8,000 strong and would enjoy gunfire support provided by the Royal Navy, so should have experienced no difficulty in taking an objective held by just 1,000 men. That it failed so dismally simply reflected the personalities of the opposing commanders. Commanding Force B was Major General A. E. Aitken, whose plan of attack lacked any means of controlling his troops once they had been committed and had been drawn up without any detailed reconnaissance of the enemy's positions. The naval gunfire support, provided by the cruiser HMS *Fox*, seemed to lack specific targets and central control and, in the event, was directed at both sides. Commanding the colony's German and native troops was one of the most remarkable officers possessed by either side in the war. Colonel Paul Emil von Lettow-Vorbeck differed considerably in his outlook from the contemporary generation of German officers although, like them, he had graduated from Imperial Germany's system of cadet academies. However, the ambition of most officers was to pass through the stages of regimental life with the object of obtaining a staff appointment and because of this service abroad was unpopular since it removed them from the mainstream of military life. Lettow-Vorbeck, however, took a contrary view. He enjoyed the experience of practical soldiering which could only be had in Germany's colonies and had already served in China during the Boxer Rebellion and in South West Africa against the Hereros, while in Tanga colony he had built up a formidable force of *Schutztruppe* battalions.

Once ashore, Force B's advance was quickly brought to a standstill. Under fire for the first time and attacked by thousands of bees whose nests had been destroyed by rifle and machine-gun fire, most of the Indian units fled, leaving the Loyals and the Kashmir Rifles to hold the line under increasing pressure. By 4 November most of the landing force was scrambling aboard anything that would float and take them out to their transports. The Loyals, their discipline intact, were holding the perimeter of the beachhead but as the time for their own embarkation approached they were specifically ordered not to bring out their machine guns with them. The order provoked disgust and contempt, but it was an order just the same and had to be obeyed. When the final cost of the disaster was established, it seemed that Force B's casualties amounted to 800 killed, 500 wounded and several hundreds more missing and probably in the enemy's hands. Amongst the abandoned equipment were a dozen machine guns, many hundred discarded rifles, 600,000 rounds of ammunition and huge quantities of clothing and blankets that had been unloaded during the early hours of the landing. To no one's surprise, Aitken's court martial dealt with him severely, depriving him of his command, reducing his rank by two steps and placing him on half-pay for the remainder of the war. As for Lettow-Vorbeck, he now possessed sufficient arms, ammunition and equipment to carry on a guerrilla campaign that, thanks to Force B's debacle, had been extended far beyond his original estimates.

Curiously, the episode seems to have worried the British public less than the fact that on 20 September a British cruiser, HMS *Pegasus*, had been surprised and sunk in Zanzibar harbour by the recently arrived German cruiser SMS *Konigsberg* without scoring a single hit on her opponent. In fact, the result of the duel should have surprised no one as *Pegasus*, launched in 1898, had formed part of Queen Victoria's navy and, like many of the Royal Navy's numerous elderly warships, was deployed on distant stations while the more formidable modern elements of the fleet were retained in home waters as a defence against Germany's High Seas Fleet. Added to this, *Pegasus* was undergoing a boiler clean, most of her fires were out, her eight 4-inch guns were seriously outranged by the modern *Konigsberg*'s ten 4.1-inch gun armament, and the outcome can be seen as a foregone conclusion. What caused most concern was the fact that *Konigsberg* was operating close to the southern exit of the Red Sea, which was itself part of the British Empire's imperial lifeline. In addition, a second modern German cruiser, the *Emden*, was already engaged in a destructive career stretching from the East Indies to the Bay of Bengal that was causing insurance rates to rocket. It can thus be seen that the need to secure the seas possessed a higher priority than the prosecution of a minor colonial campaign. In the event, while serious, the situation was not quite as threatening as might have been feared, for immediately after leaving Zanzibar *Konigsberg* went into hiding in the complex delta of the Rufiji river. Having been detected, she remained bottled up there until she was sunk by the gunfire of the monitors HMS *Mersey* and *Severn* on 11 July 1915, corrections to their fall of shot being signalled by aircraft. In the meantime, *Emden* had been intercepted and sunk by HMAS *Sydney* at the Cocos Islands on 4 November 1914, although some of her crew managed to reach home after an epic series of adventures.

Following his successful defence of Tanga, Lettow-Vorbeck took the initiative and led his *Schutztruppe* to the frontier with Kenya, which at that time was known as British East Africa. He marched as far north as Serengeti, to the east of Mount Kilimanjaro, pushing out patrols as far as Voi, and embarked on a campaign of raids against the Uganda Railway, which connected that territory with Mombasa on the coast. Regular attacks were made on repair and construction gangs who were kept busy because of damage caused to the track during the hours of darkness. Lack of resources forced the local British commander, Brigadier General Michael Tighe, to fight a defensive war although as soon as adequate reinforcements arrived he planned to extend the railway southwards from Voi to link up with the German line from Tanga to Moshi.

With the arrival of Lieutenant Nalder and his four cars, the situation underwent a radical change. The first task given to the cars was to patrol the line as far as its railhead. For much of its route it had been cut through thick bush which imposed serious limits on visibility and therefore made life much easier for the enemy's raiding parties. A road was therefore cut and levelled beside the track. After the first encounters between the cars and the raiders the latter quickly developed the same sort of superstitious terror whenever they appeared that attacks on the line soon ceased.

When the line reached Maktau an entrenched camp was constructed and cars continued their patrols in conjunction with mounted infantry. The object was to prevent the enemy approaching the British positions, but within this context considerable cunning was employed. Obviously the cars could not employ their speed in this type of bush, so they were deployed in positions against which the mounted infantry drove any raiding party they encountered, and the car's machine guns did the rest. To achieve this kind of deployment the cars were frequently compelled to leave the track and take to the bush with all its numerous invisible pitfalls for wheeled vehicles. On one occasion a car completely overturned when its nearside front wheel fell into an invisible ant-bear hole, yet despite this mishap it was extracted the following morning and continued with the task in hand.

Naturally, as the company's history of Rolls Royce cars during the Great War relates:

the Germans were desperately anxious to find a counter to the cars which were spoiling their guerrilla tactics. All sorts of booby traps were laid for the cars. Mines were laid on the tracks they used; game pits dug in the hope that the cars would fall into them; and on the main 'road' to Taveta trenches were echeloned half

across the track at intervals of a few yards so that there was not
room for the cars to get enough lock on the steering wheels to go
round without considerable manoeuvre. Several times, when the
presence of these traps delayed the cars, the latter were rushed by
the enemy but never with any success, and they generally incurred
more or less severe loss for their pains.

The history also makes the point that despite the cars being in action so
frequently that the crews were unable to carry out the recommended
maintenance programme, such was the quality of the engineering that
went into their construction that they were not off the road for a single
day.

At the beginning of 1916 Tighe was reinforced by the first South
African contingents to reach the theatre. Shortly after, the cars played
a notable part in the storming and capture of the enemy's fortified
camp at Serengeti, driving right up to the enemy trenches which they
enfiladed with machine-gun fire. However, a few days later an attack on
the enemy-held Salaita Hill came close to ending in disaster.

One of the South African brigades suddenly found itself, while in
the act of deploying, under heavy machine-gun fire from trenches
artfully concealed in the bush and, while the brigade was trying to
reform, the enemy heavily counter-attacked, with the result that
the South Africans were compelled to retire. It was during this
phase of the fight that two of the cars effected a brilliant little
enterprise which saved the infantry from incurring far more
serious losses than they did. These two cars made their way in
by a narrow bush track and actually got in rear of the German
trenches, which they swept with machine-gun fire until the water
jackets of their guns were shot through and disabled, and only
managed to get out by a piece of the sheerest good fortune. The
track by which they had got into position could not be found,
and to get through thick bush was out of the question but, just as

the gallant crews had given up hope, the path was discovered and the cars withdrew in time to play a splendid part in covering the retirement of the brigade.

After this the rainy season put a stop to serious campaigning until the end of April. General Jan Smuts was now in overall command and his strategic aim was a thrust from Arusha to Kilimatinde on the Tanga Central Railway. This would be carried out by a column led by Brigadier General van Deventer and effectively isolate von Lettow-Vorbeck's troops in the north unless they withdrew quickly. Meanwhile, Lieutenant Nalder's cars had spent the rainy season at Mbuyuni where the crews were able to get some rest and carry out some much needed maintenance. Two of the Army's Armoured Motor Batteries, each of four cars, had arrived in East Africa. Although Nalder and his men still belonged to the RNACD, for the sake of convenience all three units were placed under the command of Colonel Sir John Willoughby.

Immediately upon landing, the first of the new arrivals was directed to join van Deventer by sea. It was hoped that by doing so it might reach its destination before the rains broke and, had it not been for its transport echelon, it would have succeeded. It took over five weeks to cover the sixty-mile stretch of the route between Moshi and Arusha. The transport lorries stalled on the most modest gradients and bogged down in every riverbed, so that the armoured cars were constantly hauling them out of trouble. On the third day the rains broke and the road became virtually impassable. For the next month officers and men worked like slaves to keep the battery moving, despite an outbreak of fever and dysentery. At Kidjenge swamp, just a few hundred yards across, the four cars were hauled through in a day, assisted by gangs of natives hauling on ropes, although the driving wheels, spinning in liquid mud, actually put an additional six miles on each mileometer! Again, when one of the cars broke through a crust of mud into the clinging bed of a sunken river, not even the combined efforts of thirty-two oxen could move the vehicle one inch until, an hour later, fresh rain liquefied the thick, black, adhesive sludge. And so on – although by now the reader will have gathered that armoured-car soldiering in East Africa was not a soft option. Incredibly, the Rolls Royce armoured cars finished the ordeal in full working order.

The third battery was referred to briefly in C. R. Kutz's book *War on Wheels* in which he wrote, 'Captain Brown of the heavy armoured car battery was placed in charge of "public gardens and Government Farm" when his cars came to the limit of passable roads'. The word heavy suggests the same type of vehicle that Commander Locker Lampson's unit put to such good use in Russia and it seems probable that Captain Kutz, a serving officer of the United States Army writing in 1940, is pointing out as politely as possible the absurdity of military bureaucrats despatching types of vehicle to theatres of war in which they cannot possibly operate.

Notwithstanding the difficulties experienced along the route of van Deventer's thrust, his advance changed the character of the war in East Africa. Now in serious danger of being isolated, von Lettow-Vorbeck, whose strength never exceeded 3,000 German officers and under-officers and 11,000 native *askaris*, lacked the resources to fight anything more than a guerrilla campaign and withdrew steadily southwards. On the way he picked up several of the *Konigsberg*'s 4.1-inch and 3.5-inch guns that had been salvaged from the wreck and provided with travelling carriages constructed for them at the railway workshops in Dar es Salaam, plus shells brought ashore from a blockade runner run aground on the coast, acquisitions providing him with a heavy punch that astonished his opponents. Once he had crossed the Rufiji river he represented no further danger to British East Africa and continued south to harry Portuguese East Africa to the verge of disintegration, this being a colony of England's oldest ally.

Virtually nothing remained for Willoughby's cars to do in East Africa. In response to the need for armoured cars elsewhere, they were despatched to Egypt, Mespotamia, Arabia and Salonika where fresh adventures awaited them.

Chapter 8

The Land of the Two Rivers

Sometimes known as the Land of the Two Rivers, at others as The Cradle of Civilisation, as Mesopotamia in 1914 and today as Iraq, it would have been of little or no interest to Great Britain in 1914 had not huge quantities of fuel oil been discovered there and in neighbouring Persia, today known as Iran, for the Royal Navy had initiated a change-over from coal firing to oil induction and could not take the chance of letting these rich supplies fall into the hands of the Central Powers. Both countries shipped the bulk of their oil in tankers, first down the Shatt al Arab waterway, in which the Tigris and Euphrates rivers merged their waters for their final journey into the Persian Gulf and beyond, although some Persian oil was actually loaded aboard tankers at locations in the Gulf itself.

Securing possession of the oil was as important as denying it to the enemy, but a major problem existed in that Mesopotamia already formed part of the Ottoman Empire. Urgent necessity therefore demanded a rapid occupation of the country's oil producing and shipping assets and, in view of India's proximity to what had by default become a war zone, the Indian Government was made responsible for the task. In November 1914 both the Shatt al Arab waterway and the southern city of Basra were captured without undue difficulty. Little resistance was offered by the enemy's troops, giving a false impression of the quality of the remainder of the Turkish Army, whereas the truth was that the locally recruited Arab soldiery felt little if any loyalty to the decadent Sultanate and its administration in Constantinople.

The over-optimistic decision was therefore taken to despatch a force up the Tigris with the object of capturing Baghdad. This was commanded by Major General Sir Charles Townshend, a narcissistic officer who had previously taken part in the Battle of Omdurman and wallowed in the praise showered on him for the successful defence of Chitral Fort on the northern frontier of India. The problem was that while Charlie Townshend might be a good soldier he was his own worst enemy, a man with a keen interest in theatricals who saw himself as always playing the major role and receiving the greatest adulation during the curtain calls. For his long advance up the river Tigris he was given a flotilla of Royal Navy gunboats and an assortment of craft containing infantry, artillery and two armoured cars, possibly Fiats armoured in India, of which little is known. Mile after mile passed by with little or no incident. The troops, officers and men alike found that with the exception of the palm trees, agricultural plots and the occasional villages bordering the river, the country was a dun-coloured featureless waste with almost no features that would assist offensive or defensive tactics. Yet, while the desert might look empty, it was home to particularly venomous tribes of Bedouin who, throughout the country's history, had robbed, stripped and murdered anyone they came across to their hearts' content, including merchants, travellers and even harmless archaeologists. In the present circumstances, sniping at small bodies of troops became a new sport, although any form of pursuit would quickly see them vanish into infinity. Those forced to soldier in Mesopotamia faced temperatures that could soar to 120 degrees, clouds of flies and swarms of mosquitoes that rose at dusk to bite, torment and infect with cholera and dysentery, draining away the strength of every unit they visited.

Townshend travelled so far and so fast, taking the small and rather dirty town of Kut-al-Amara on the way, that his advance became known as Townshend's Regatta. At this point Townshend warned his immediate superior, Lieutenant General Sir John Nixon, that to go further entailed serious risk, pointing out that he was now some 380 miles from the sea with just two divisions, one of which of necessity was engaged in protecting his line of communication, and that the seasonal fall of the river was making water transport difficult. He regarded retreat as unthinkable but recommended consolidation of his present position, adding that a further advance on Baghdad would require a full corps to achieve success. Nixon considered that Townshend was simply angling for promotion and ordered him to continue with what he had got, namely the 6th Indian Infantry Division and a cavalry brigade. In this he had the backing of the Commander-in-Chief India, General Sir Beauchamp Duff.

However, while Townshend spent several weeks making his preparations, no fewer than 30,000 good quality Turkish troops were streaming through Baghdad under the experienced command of Khalil Pasha. In addition, the German Field Marshal von der Goltz had been appointed as the Ottoman Empire's Commander-in-Chief in Mesopotamia. Just how much of these developments had reached Nixon is uncertain, for even though Townshend was now marching into a hornets' nest he declined to reverse his decision.

At Ctesiphon, some thirty miles from Baghdad, Townshend found the Turks entrenched on both banks of the Tigris. The ground on the right bank was impassable in places, restricting his options to a frontal assault on two lines of carefully concealed trenches, plus an attempt to turn the enemy's left flank with a flying column consisting of a cavalry brigade, an infantry battalion and two Fiat armoured cars under the command of Major General Charles Melliss, his second-in-command. Had it succeeded, this would have proved to be the battle's decisive stroke but, by the time fighting commenced on 22 November, the enemy's position had been extended and the gap no longer existed, save for an exit through which Turkish cavalry and Arab horsemen mounted a counter-attack. Neither had the stomach for this kind of close quarter melee with professionals and their enthusiasm melted away as the Fiats pumped a steady stream of heavy 0.45-calibre rounds from their early Maxim machine guns into their ranks from a flank. They turned tail, but the chance of turning the Turkish left by surprise had gone and the remainder of the battle consisted of a bloody infantry combat in which the first line of enemy trenches was captured, but not the second. With the fight still raging, Townshend ordered his soldier-servant to fetch him a change of clothes, an order that involved the man making two journeys across a still very active battlefield. Perhaps, as the general stripped and donned fresh silk undergarments, clean tunic and trousers, he thought he was giving an admirable demonstration of *sangfroid* in the presence of the enemy. With so many of his soldiers lying dead, dying or desperately wounded, others saw it very differently.

The following day the Turks counter-attacked in the hope of recovering their forward trenches. They were beaten off and finally withdrew from their positions, having sustained 6,200 casualties. Townshend could claim a victory, but he had sustained 4,600 casualties out of the 11,000 engaged and was now desperately short of ammunition. When, on 25 November, his air reconnaissance reported fresh Turkish formations streaming out of Baghdad, he accepted that the time had come for him to withdraw. His retreat was covered by the river gunboats and the cavalry brigade. On 1 December, however, the Turks caught up with him at Umm-al-Tubal and attempted to fix him in position while they turned his open desert flank, a failed attempt that cost them 1,500 casualties as opposed to 500 British. The following day Townshend reached Kut-al-Amara where his troops were able to snatch a brief rest. Put briefly, his desire for self-advertisement clouded his judgement and led him to signal Nixon to the effect that he intended to defend Kut just as he had defended Chitral. In other words, he intended letting himself be trapped although far better defensive positions existed downstream. Chitral Charlie was going to be famous again as Townshend of Kut. Perhaps the most dishonest part of this is that the Turks did not isolate Kut until 7 December. The cavalry brigade had left the town the previous day and encountered no serious difficulties. In passing, it seems probable that the Fiat armoured cars went with them as they do not appear in any account of the siege or the final stages of the Turkish advance.

Townshend had sent his wounded downriver aboard the steamer *Mejidieh* with two iron barges in tow. It took several days for the convoy to reach Basra, where its arrival created a national scandal and led to a commission of inquiry. Surrounded by a cloud of flies, dead, dying and wounded were packed so tightly together that the few medical orderlies could hardly move among them. Over all hung a dreadful smell of uncleared excrement, urine and gangrene from untreated wounds. The distribution of infected water had ensured that cholera and dysentery were rampant. Many who had survived the voyage died shortly after. All that can be said of this unspeakable episode is that it led to a dramatic improvement in the campaign's medical services.

Among those now trapped in Kut-al-Amara was Major General Melliss, who had become too ill to travel further. Melliss was a plain, honest soldier who had won the Victoria Cross during the Ashanti War and was always concerned for the welfare of his soldiers. Before Kut was isolated he managed to write a letter to his wife, revealing his contempt for most of the British generals in Mesopotamia, and Townshend in particular.

> Townshend is a hopeless incapable dreamer and an ass – vain as a peacock and full of military history comparisons, but as a practical soldier one's grandmother would be as good. Sometimes one doesn't know whether to laugh or cry at his incapacity – he never goes near his men or rarely – never goes near the front line of trenches & sees things for himself. But he is not the only rotter – there are several in high places.

On 24 December the Turks attempted to storm the town but sustained such heavy casualties that von der Goltz forbade any further such attempts and decided that he would starve the garrison into surrender, simultaneously blocking any attempt at relief. In this the geography and the seasonal rise of the river assisted him, for on the left bank of the Tigris the only approach to the town from the south lay along a narrow neck of land between the river and an extensive salt marsh in which movement was impossible, while on the right bank were numerous canals which in this, the rainy season, were serious obstacles to movement. This constriction was known as the Hannah Defile and would acquire a venomous reputation during the months ahead.

To emphasise the drama of his situation, Townshend falsely claimed that his rations would run out in a month's time. Nixon therefore ordered Lieutenant General Sir Fenton Aylmer VC, commanding the relief force, to initiate breakthrough attempts before he was ready. Needless to say, they failed. Aylmer's requests that his attacks should coincide with breakout attempts by the Kut garrison were ignored as, understandably, were Townshend's repeated requests for promotion. The garrison was in radio contact with Nixon's headquarters which put an end to the latter by signalling that Aylmer had been replaced by Major General Sir George Gorringe who had been promoted to the rank of lieutenant general. Gorringe had originally commanded the small division that had been responsible for protecting Townshend's line of communication during his initial advance and had never been considered to be a serious rival by him. When told of the promotion, Townshend burst into tears in front of an astonished junior officer.

In the meantime the commission of inquiry had seen to it that a number of chickens had come home to roost. In London the government was extremely angry that a comparatively minor operation undertaken at the request of the Admiralty had been allowed to develop into a new war front, equally angry at the way operations were being conducted by senior Indian Army officers who now found themselves staring a serious defeat in the face, and horrified by the mismanagement and inefficiency of the medical services that had brought the horrors of the *Mejidieh* into being. From now on, it would be the War Office and not the India Office that controlled operations in Mesopotamia. Nixon was dismissed, his place being taken by General Sir Percy Lake. Unable to live with the shame of what had occurred, Beauchamp Duff took his own life.

The Kut garrison's food supply did not develop serious shortages until early April 1916. Townshend's request for re-supply by air was granted but the daily delivery failed to equal the level of consumption. On 24 April the steamer *Julnur* attempted a suicidal run past the Turkish lines with fresh supplies but was driven aground by the enemy's guns. Thus far, abortive attempts to relieve the 13,000 men holding Kut had cost 23,000 casualties in the fierce fighting to break through the Hannah Defile. It would have been criminal lunacy to have continued. On the night of the *Julnur*'s loss Lord Kitchener signalled Lake to the effect that further effort would not be justified and that unless he and his senior officers held different views he was authorised to open negotiations with the enemy.

When Townshend was informed of the decision early on 26 April it was typical of him that he should blame the relief force, which had done the dying for him. Von der Goltz had died of cholera some days previously so he arranged a meeting with Khalil aboard the latter's launch. He offered £1 million in gold in exchange for the garrison's parole and the surrender of its guns. Khalil consulted his superiors in Constantinople but they would have none of it, even when the offer of gold was doubled. What they wanted was the famous General Townshend and his men as trophies, although they were willing to exchange 345 hospital cases for the same number of fit prisoners. His garrison, he was told, would be treated as 'honoured guests'. Ever the actor, he declaimed, 'I must go into captivity with my troops, even though the heat will kill me.' Instead, he spent the remainder of the war in a luxurious villa on a pleasant, breeze-cooled island in the Sea of Marmara. The remainder of the Turks' 'honoured guests' were sent to prison camps where 7,000 of them died from starvation, malnutrition, disease, lack of medical facilities and the brutal indifference of their guards. Some of those who did survive owed their lives to Melliss, who was too ill to travel when the main body of the garrison was marched off. He left Kut some days later and almost immediately began to encounter the bodies of half-starved British and Indian soldiers who simply died where they had collapsed or were barely alive. He insisted that his Turkish guards place the latter aboard his convoy's vehicles and the Turks, shrugging, did so. As the months in captivity passed, Townshend was urged to visit his men in their camps to verify their conditions. He never did so, thereby provoking a formal complaint from Melliss to the War Office.

Following the surrender of Kut the Mesopotamian front remained quiet for several months. The Russians had made some advances into Asia Minor and North Persia and, to counter these, Khalil, who had developed a poor opinion of the British soldier, withdrew many of his troops from the Tigris, leaving just three divisions to hold the line under Kiazim Karabekir. The British, on the other hand, were grimly determined to avenge their defeat and were steadily increasing both the size of their army and the quality of its equipment. Lake was relieved by Lieutenant General Sir Frederick Maude in August. Maude had the reputation of possessing a cold and uncommunicative personality and had a tendency to meddle in the detailed internal workings of his subordinate formations, a habit unlikely to earn one friends. Against this, he was a sound strategist and a good administrator who left little to chance. He knew what he wanted to do, and that was to fight a war of movement in which his opponents would be unable to respond. In order to achieve this he knew that he would require a sound logistic infrastructure if lasting successes were to be consolidated. This approach to his problems found favour with the War Office which willingly supplied most of what he asked for. A narrow-gauge railway was constructed from Qurna to Amara (and extended to Baghdad in the fullness of time). This was policed by the Railway Armoured Motor Battery consisting of the original Fiat armoured cars, joined later by more up to date twin-turreted Austins, both types being adapted for railway work by the fitting of flanged wheels. Simultaneously, a squadron of P-class shallow-draught river steamers, specially designed for supply duties with the Army, reached the Tigris, as did a flotilla of modern gunboats. The strength of the army was increased to two corps and a cavalry division, with an enlarged artillery element.

In the days when the India Office was responsible for running the campaign it had relied on plodding animal transport that consumed huge quantities of fodder that had to be shipped from India. This was an absurd situation when the army was serving in one of the world's most important sources of fuel oil and lubricants. This was immediately apparent to those engaged in the overall programme planning of reconstruction prior to returning to the offensive. Taking the nature of the terrain into account, it was decided to invest in a large purchase of Ford Model Ts, which were reliable and possessed sufficient ground clearance. Their use, however, was not to be confined to the carriage of cargo and they were increasingly used in the lorried infantry role, simultaneously increasing the infantry's operational mobility and saving it from much stamina-consuming marching under a baking sun. The dramatic nature of the change is revealed by the fact that at the beginning of Maude's planned offensive his motor transport fleet consisted of 100 heavy lorries, while at the end of the war no fewer than 7,000 vehicles were available.

The army was further modernised by the arrival of six LAMBs (Light Armoured Motor Batteries). No. 6 had originally served in Salonika with just two Rolls Royces. It was withdrawn to Egypt in May 1917 and joined by two more Rolls Royces and the four Leylands of No. 1 (Willoughby's) Armoured Motor Battery. The latter, as their nomenclature suggests, had served in German East Africa, but none too successfully as their weight, in excess of three tons, combined with narrow tyre tracks had combined to rut the more primitive tracks too deeply for general use. Nevertheless, their design did contain some interesting features, including a rear-facing machine gun in a limited traverse mounting, and a rear steering wheel that could be useful if the need arose to get out of trouble quickly. The unit reached Mesopotamia in August 1917 and discarded its Leylands the following month.

Having served in France, No. 7 LAMB reached Mesopotamia in February 1918. One source suggests that at this period it had only two cars, quite possibly Rolls Royces, although in November-December

1918 it is on record as having taken over some of Duncars' Austins – see below.

No. 8 LAMB also served in France and was equipped with four Rolls Royces and two towed 3-pounder guns. It absorbed the similarly equipped No. 9 LAMB in October 1917 and the combined unit reached Mesopotamia in December of that year.

Nos. 13 and 14 LAMBs served in the UK, reaching Mesopotamia respectively in December 1916 and January 1917. Each of these units was equipped with eight Rolls Royces from the outset.

No. 15 LAMB. Formed in Egypt in January 1917 as No. 17 Motor Machine Gun Battery and equipped with five Studebaker cars mounting machine guns. Served Palestine April 1917, transferred to Mesopotamia in August 1917 and changed title.

Two larger armoured car formations, Duncars and Norperforce, were formed towards the end of the campaign and their operations are discussed later in this chapter.

Meanwhile, to return to the situation developing at the Hannah Defile during the mid-winter of 1916, a very worried Kiazim Karabekir, fully aware of the dramatic changes taking place in Maude's army, signalled Khalil requesting urgent reinforcement. The latter, fully committed to events in Persia, returned a blunt reply, commenting that the positions downstream from Kut had proved impregnable in the past and would do so again in the future. He would have felt a great deal less secure if he had read the thoughts running through Maude's mind.

Maude was aware that Kiazim had already deployed his whole command well forward and had nothing left in reserve. The bulk of the Turkish strength was still concentrated in the narrow neck of land on the left bank of the river. On the right bank the defences were less formidable and had been allowed to run down. He decided to eliminate these one at a time, working his way slowly and steadily upstream past Kut, and then cross to the left bank. Unless Kiazim had been blessed with the foresight to withdraw in good time, the consequences of Maude's indirect approach would be to trap him.

The British offensive commenced on 13 December with a feint attack on the Turks' left bank positions. The strength of the attackers' bombardment and the manner in which the attack itself was pressed home caused Kiazim sufficient alarm to shift troops across from the right bank. In this manner the pressure was maintained for several weeks until Turkish nerves in the Hannah Defile were broken by sustained shelling from the south and across the river. By the third week of February Maude's advance on the right bank had reached a point several miles north of Kut. Those Turks still holding their original front in the defile would have been less than human if they were not given nervously to glancing over their shoulders at what had become enemy territory. On 23 February they were finally driven out of their trenches. Unfortunately for them, Kiazim's decision to abandon Kut had been made too late for, on that very day, Maude's 14th Division crossed the river at the Shumran Bend and put in place a pontoon bridge. The following day the cavalry crossed to find Kiazim's troops streaming across the neck of the peninsula, covered by a strong flank guard. This was withdrawn during the night and the following day Maude's cavalry and the armoured cars became the spearhead of the British advance. Once again and for the last time the Turkish rearguard made a stand, but pulled out after dark.

The 26th of February was remarkable for a naval battle fought between three British gunboats HMS *Tarantula*, *Mantis* and *Moth* and an equal number of Turkish gunboats. Two of the Turkish craft were sunk and the third – originally HMS *Firefly* – was driven aground. She had also grounded and been abandoned during Townshend's retreat from Ctesiphon and was now able to resume her career in King George's navy. At the Nahr Kellek Bend *Tarantula*, *Mantis* and *Moth* caught up with the enemy's marching column. What followed lay somewhere between a massacre and a rout. The gunboats opened up with their main armament and automatic weapons. As men fell in their dozens the column burst apart to become a horde of running, terrified men seeking safety in the desert. There was none to be found for soon the cavalry and the armoured cars reached the scene and weary legs could never out-distance a galloping horseman's sword let alone the Maxim bullet stream. Many flung down their weapons in the hope that their surrender would be accepted. In fact, over 4,000 Turkish prisoners had been taken since the crossing of the Tigris and it was obvious that Kiazim's army had reached the point of complete disintegration. Its dead, wounded and the wreckage of war covered every mile of the road – abandoned guns, smashed carts, military equipment of every kind, live shells, office furniture, papers, books and even a fine new Mercedes tourer, its tanks drained of fuel.

Maude halted for several days at Aziziyeh to allow his supplies to catch up. On 5 March he resumed his advance to discover that the Turks had tried to form a new front at Lujj. This was probed by the Cavalry Division and abandoned during the night. The next day the troopers rode across the now-deserted and silent battlefield of Ctesiphon and by the evening of the 7th had reached the banks of the Diyala, a tributary of the Tigris that flowed in from the north–east. On the distant horizon could be seen the domes and minarets of the army's long-sought objective, the city of Baghdad itself.

It was decided to employ the tactics against Baghdad that had been used so successfully against Kut. The 13th Division crossed the Diyala to mount a holding attack while the Cavalry Division and two infantry brigades re-crossed the Tigris and began advancing up its right bank to by-pass the city. The Turks were offering a stubborn resistance but Khalil was seriously unsettled by the Cavalry Division's threat to his rear and managed to squeeze out of the trap that was closing around him. On 11 March a cavalry patrol entered the railway station and was informed that the Turks had left and were retreating northwards. Maude entered the city some hours later to find that the city of the Caliphs was somewhat grubbier than its distant view or the *Tales of the Arabian Nights* might suggest. The city's civilian administrators requested assistance in dealing with a plague of looters, which was readily given, and the Union Flag was raised over the city hall. The loss of Baghdad was a crushing blow to Turkish prestige throughout the Muslim world. An attempt to recapture the city was made by Ali Ishan Pasha's Turkish XIII Corps advancing down the Diyala from Persia but this was defeated in a series of engagements at Delli Abbas, forcing Ali Ishan to withdraw through Jebel Hamrin. Maude captured Samarra on 24 April. After this, the sweltering onset of the hot season ended operations for several months. Maude died from cholera on 18 November. Despite his reserve, his death was deeply regretted by his officers and men alike. He was not only respected for his sound instincts as a general, but also liked for his real concern for his soldiers and their conditions and his prompt reward for any outstanding act of bravery.

His successor was Lieutenant General Sir William Marshall, who was forced to conduct a war of offensive defence because of changed strategic priorities. Because of British successes in Palestine, detailed in a later chapter, the Turks were forced to reinforce that theatre rather than Mesopotamia, while the collapse of Russia following the Revolution forced Marshall to send British reinforcements to the Russian troops trying to prevent a Turkish seizure of the Baku oilfields, a difficult operation involving a line of communications stretching across northern Persia and the Caspian Sea.

In the meantime, Marshall employed mobile battle groups consisting of cavalry, LAMBs and motorised infantry riding in Fords and sometimes horse-drawn artillery batteries and engineer units to conduct his offensive–defence operations. Of these, by far the most successful was carried out against a Turkish force holding Khan al Baghdadi on the Euphrates. In command was Major General Sir H. T. Brooking of the 15th Division who had at his disposal 11 Cavalry Brigade, three LAMBs, two-and-a-half infantry brigades riding in Ford vans, and supporting artillery. Before the main attack went in, the cavalry and LAMBs had worked their way round the enemy's right flank under cover of darkness and established themselves across the Aleppo road behind the Wadi Hauran. When Brooking's infantry stormed Khan al Baghdadi on 26 March 1918 the Turks attempted to withdraw but found their only avenue of retreat effectively barred and surrendered *en masse*. The cavalry and the armoured cars then set off on a ruthless exploitation along the Aleppo road. The cars quickly took the lead and, shortly after dawn on the 28th, the 8th LAMB under Captain D. Tod entered the village of 'Anah. There, Tod was informed that two British officer prisoners and their escort had left two hours previously. Tod reported the situation and was told that the two were almost certainly Colonel J. E. Tennant, commander of the Royal Flying Corps in Mesopotamia, and Major P. C. S. Hobart of the Bengal Sappers and Miners, whose aircraft had been shot down while flying over Khan al Baghdadi on 25 March. Tod was ordered to pursue to a distance of 100 miles if necessary and told that aircraft would supply him if his fuel ran low. He caught up with the party just thirty-two miles from 'Anah and freed the prisoners at a moment when the escort's attitude had become dangerously threatening. He was obviously beginning to enjoy himself and took advantage of the long-range ticket he had been given, continuing his foray into the enemy's rear areas for a further forty miles. By the time he returned to his own lines he had captured an assortment of bewildered Turkish and German notables and their interesting papers. The episode almost certainly influenced Hobart in his decision to transfer to the Tank Corps in 1923 and it will be remembered that it was he who not only prepared the legendary 7th Armoured Division for desert warfare but also trained the 79th Armoured Division which, at the time, was the largest assault engineering formation in the world.

Chapter 9

The Road Past Moses' Rock

Meanwhile, a thoroughly experienced unit was about to return to the fray. With the exception of regular naval officers and warrant officers who returned to their own service, the majority of Locker Lampson's unit was recalled from leave in January 1918, discovering that they had passed from Admiralty to Army control and now belonged to a formation of the Motor Machine Gun Corps. Smiles took over as second-in-command with the rank of lieutenant colonel; Wells Hood, Ruston and Scott, the Staff Surgeon, became majors; the senior lieutenants became captains; and a handful of suitable warrant officers were commissioned as second lieutenants. The former petty officers became warrant officers, staff sergeants and sergeants according to their experience and their officers' recommendations. As ranks in the Royal Navy and the Army were not precisely equivalent, rates of pay were suitably adjusted so that no one suffered from the transfer.

On 28 January the unit embarked at Southampton on the first leg of a journey that would have stretched the travel resources of the Thomas Cook organisation. On arrival at Cherbourg the men boarded a train that transported them across France and Italy to Taranto. The troopship *Malwa* transported them to Alexandria, which they reached on 15 February. They then travelled by train to Port Suez where the steamer *Nile* was waiting to embark them for the sweltering voyage down the Red Sea, across the Indian Ocean, into the Persian Gulf, from whence the *Nile* entered the Tigris to disembark at Basra, outside which the unit was accommodated in mud huts.

The personnel from the Kursk depot party rejoined in May, but there was still one prominent name missing from the unit's present nominal roll and it was that of Locker Lampson himself. Illness had prevented him travelling and in a moving gesture he had written personally to every man who served under him in Russia thanking him for his services and, entirely out of his own pocket, presenting each of them with a 15-shilling savings certificate to be held in trust for their return. He would certainly have been a difficult commander to follow but his successor, a Colonel Crawford, an immensely tall Indian cavalry officer, knew nothing about his new command and had made no effort to find out. On first addressing the brigade he commented that no one had heard of them, and since they were headed for the back of beyond in Trans-Caucasia no one was likely to, unless they did well, which was what he demanded of them. Small wonder that the expression of several hundred pairs of eyes that had hitherto contained only curiosity quickly hardened into something approaching dislike. Someone, almost certainly Smiles, quietly advised him that the men had, in fact, been involved in active operations in that area just two years previously and since then had become what was probably the most experienced armoured car unit in the British Army. Crawford's chagrin can be imagined, but the damage was done and could not be undone. This was a great pity, for he was a very capable officer with a thorough knowledge of logistics whose planning enabled the brigade to function smoothly in the most trying conditions. On the ground itself, the men would see very little of him.

The reason for the brigade being earmarked for further operations in Trans-Caucasia was simple. Following Russia's collapse all her Trans-Caucasian provinces, including the Baku oilfield, had been ceded to Turkey by the Treaty of Brest-Litovsk. The British reaction was that the Baku oil must be denied to the Central Powers at all costs. In this they were supported by the ethnic Russian population which had no intention of being ruled by Constantinople. This states the situation at its simplest, for there also existed blood feuds between Russian and Turk, Christian and Muslim, Kurd and Armenian which was further complicated by private factions of Red and White armies fighting a civil war and indulging in a little banditry on the side. In such circumstances forming any sort of stable alliance would be impossible. Marshall regarded the mission as little better than madness but he had his orders. The task was given to an Indian Army officer, Major General Lionel Dunsterville, whose personal qualities suggested that he might succeed where others would fail. At school he had shared a study with Rudyard Kipling and was the original Stalky of the latter's *Stalky & Co*. He could speak fluently in eight languages, of which five were Asian, and was endowed with considerable charm and great powers of persuasion. He was, however, well aware that he had been handed the messy end of a very dirty stick and decided to see how the land lay for himself. With a small party he made the difficult journey from Baghdad to the port of Enzeli on the south-eastern shore of the Caspian Sea. In this part of the world it was impossible to keep anything a secret for long. Enzeli, like Baku itself, was in Bolshevik hands for the moment and the Russians were well aware of his intentions. He found a blunt message from the Baku Soviet awaiting him, curtly rejecting his offers of technical assistance and, indeed, aid of any sort. He was left with no alternative other than to return to Baghdad and await the concentration of the troops which had been placed at his disposal, which would be known collectively as Dunsterforce.

The armoured car brigade formed part of this and was designated Duncars. It was forced to mark time at Basra while its cars were still at sea, weapon training, route marching and playing sport. Its official establishment was forty twin-turreted Austins, organised in five eight-car squadrons, each consisting of four two-car sections. However, when they reached Basra at the end of April it was found that sixteen of the cars had been rushed to France to assist in defeating the formidable series of offensives mounted by the German army in the spring of 1918. Consequently, only Duncars' A, B and E Squadrons were fully equipped; C and D Squadrons were re-organised as 8-gun motor machine-gun squadrons mounted on Ford or Peerless vehicles. Having checked over its vehicles, the unit proceeded upriver by barge, passing sites the names of which had been only too familiar two years previously. On 5 May Baghdad was reached and the brigade went into camp at nearby Hinadia.

There it was learned that Dunsterville planned to advance on Enzeli along the axis Baghdad-Kermanshah-Hamadan-Kasvin-Resht. His staff warned him that the Austin armoured cars and their heavy Peerless support lorries would be unable to cross a number of high mountain passes. They would have to cope with precipitous gradients, defiles barely wider than the vehicles' own widths, innumerable fords that had never been intended for use by mechanical transport, narrow mountain ledges bordered by sheer drops of several thousand feet, variations in temperature between blistering heat and, in the highest parts of the route, frost, snow, thin air and cold so intense that sleep was impossible. Crawford, with the support of his officers, agreed that the obstacles were formidable but not beyond the capacity of the vehicles or their drivers. The first to be tackled was the Pai Tak Pass, halfway up which was a triumphal arch erected by Alexander the Great to commemorate his victory over King Darius. The climb was long and hard but as nothing in comparison to what followed. Two more passes had to be climbed before Kermanshah was reached, the Khurkur (6,000 feet) and the Kuh-e-Safid (4,000 feet). At Bisotun, beyond Kermanshah, a huge panel carved into a rock face depicted Darius dealing with lesser kings. Below this, a stream flowed out of a fissure in the cliff. Some of the men, with memories of Sunday school, named it Moses' Rock, for when water was desperately needed, Moses had struck a rock with his staff and had not water gushed out? It was pointless to argue that the great man had never been within many hundred miles of the site; Moses' Rock was as good a name as any to mark the location on one's map. From the outset, it had been apparent that the distance, in excess of 400 miles, would be the major determining factor on how the operation would be conducted. The entire area was in such a state of unrest that, as far as Duncars was concerned, only Major Ruston's A Squadron would be going the whole way. The two remaining armoured car squadrons would ensure that the route remained open while the Lewis-gun squadrons became responsible for the security of supply dumps that were established along the way.

At Hamadan, where food was so scare it was said that cases of cannibalism had been reported, the force encountered a brigade of Cossacks under a Colonel Bicherakov, the last Russian commander remaining on Persian soil. Bicherakov was loyal to the old St Petersburg regime and detested Bolshevism. His ambition, and that of his men, was to join one of the White armies fighting in Russia, and to that end they were also marching to Enzeli. All had gone well until, halfway between Kasvin and Resht, further progress was blocked by some 5,000 natives of Gilan Province holding an entrenched position on a ridge overlooking a vital bridge at Menjil. In command was a local warlord named Mirza Kuchik Khan who was presently playing the part of a Turkish irregular with a German officer to advise him. Bicherakov was informed by the latter that Kuchik Khan would allow the Russians to proceed in small groups. As far as the British were concerned, the road would remain closed. This did not suit Bicherakov, who appreciated the presence of Dunsterforce and was anxious to continue the association. He informed Dunsterville of the situation and the latter set his own troops in motion. First to join the Cossacks was Sergeant George Martin's section of Austins, followed by C Squadron 14th Hussars and two Martinsyde Scouts of No. 72 Squadron, Royal Air Force.

Bicherakov had noticed that Kuchik Khan's position was dominated by a spur of the Elburz mountain and sent up his mountain battery to occupy it. At dawn on 16 June the two aircraft buzzed the enemy trenches. The tribesmen swarmed out of them to take pot-shots at them. The Russian battery, prompted, dropped several shells among them and the Cossack infantry deployed to attack. This was too much for Kuchik Khan's army, which bolted. The cavalry, British and Cossack, swept round their right flank while the two cars raced along the road to secure the bridge, doing considerable execution in the process. 'A bit of a scrap up the road,' was Sergeant Martin's unimpressed comment, an entirely appropriate verdict from a survivor of the fighting in Romania and Galicia.

The road to Resht and Enzeli was now open. Bicherakov brigade advanced along it, holding key points until they could be handed over to Dunsterforce's advance guard which consisted of a flying column made up of various infantry detachments from the 1/4th Hampshire Regiment and 1/2nd Gurkha Rifles, and two guns of No. 8 Battery, the whole escorted by Duncars' leading squadron. Over 500 Model T Fords were required to transport the column and although the infantry dismounted to march up the worst of the passes only half remained in a serviceable condition at the end of their gruelling journey. Duncars, too was beginning to suffer from technical problems. The Austins should have been issued with two different types of tyre – normal pneumatic tyres for road use, and solid Rubberine tyres for use in action. Unfortunately, only the Rubberine tyres had reached Baghdad and the cars had made the journey on them. Rubberine was a hard composite substance that would absorb bullets, but a problem existed in that it had been designed for use in temperate climates. The long journey had included contrasting extremes of temperatures and movement along rough going. The result was that the Rubberine began to shred and break up. Fresh supplies could only be obtained from the railhead at Baghdad, a journey involving a ten-day round trip back to the brigade's forward base at Hamadan. Even then, the labour involved in replacing the worn tyres was considerable as each weighed not less than 200lbs. In one month Duncars used 75 per cent of an anticipated year's supply of Rubberines.

When his brigade approached Enzeli, Bicherakov, anxious to return his men to Russia at any cost, announced his total conversion to Bolshevism and offered to take command of operations against the Turks, who were marching on Baku along the railway line from Tiflis. The Baku Soviet, seriously alarmed, accepted his offer with alacrity and even arranged shipping for him. Dunsterville approved of this development and even attached a section of A Squadron's armoured cars for service with the Cossacks. This tiny unit, under the command of Captain Crossing, was known as No. 2 Battery and, in that it actually fought for the Bolsheviks for a while, earned the distinction of being the only British unit to do so during the period of the Intervention.

Bicherakov sailed from Enzeli with No. 2 Battery and supporting transport on 4 July and disembarked at the little harbour of Alyat, fifty miles south of Baku, that night. Contact with the enemy commenced immediately and they were in action almost continuously, covering the Russian withdrawal. The Turkish Caucasus-Islam Army was a mixed bunch, half being Turkish regulars and the rest being a mixture of Kurdish and other Muslim levies. It did not impress the British crews greatly, but it had the advantage of numbers and was able to instigate outflanking movements that compelled Bicherakov to continue his retreat. On the other hand, the Bolshevik infantry were regarded as nothing better than the dregs of Baku, driven into action by their commissars.

On 26 July Lieutenant Hull took out a reconnaissance patrol consisting of one car and two lorries. The patrol crossed a bridge over a defile, receiving assurances from the Bolshevik bridge guard commander that he would hold it until their return. He and his men vanished as soon as the Turks appeared. Neither any member of the patrol, nor any of their vehicles, was ever seen again. The probability is that they were ambushed when they returned to the bridge, having mistaken the Turks for Bolsheviks.

So far, the Baku Bolsheviks had served Bicherakov's purpose very well, but now he had no further use for them and commandeered a train, steaming off to the north on 31 July and taking No. 2 Battery with him. The slow journey along the Caspian coast through country ravaged by civil war ended at Derbent on 16 August. The Cossacks now broke out their true colours and stormed the town, forcing the local Bolsheviks to withdraw to Petrovsk. No. 2 Battery was not involved in the fighting and it seems that Bicherakov had accepted Dunsterville's point that it could be employed against the Turks, but must remain neutral as far as Russian affairs were concerned. The battery entered the town when it surrendered on 3 September and remained there for the next eight weeks, assisting in its defence against the continued Turkish advance. One of its armoured cars, considered to be beyond local repair, was shipped back to Persia. During an action on 16 October, Crossing was wounded and four of his men killed. This brought the little unit's losses to an unacceptable level, particularly as many of its members were suffering from malaria. The battery had few regrets when orders were received on 25 October to board the transport for Enzeli, taking its remaining vehicles with it.

Meanwhile, there had been a dramatic change in Dunsterforce's situation. Mirza Kuchik Khan had lost face among his followers as a result of his defeat at Menjil Bridge. By way of explanation he claimed that he had never intended to fight the Russians, whom he admired. On the other hand, his opinion of the British was that they had neither liking nor aptitude for war and would be easy prey. He therefore arranged for the ambush of a Hampshire patrol, forgetting, perhaps, that British infantry were trained to fire fifteen *aimed* rounds per minute. As a result, his ambush party had much the worse of the affair. Nothing daunted, he decided to capture Resht. If formally defended, the town would have required a defensive perimeter of seven miles. Superficially, it seemed a sensible decision as only 450 Hampshires and Gurkhas were present, supported by 8 Battery Royal Field Artillery's two guns and two Austin armoured cars belonging to Duncars' B Squadron, which had established a defensive camp on the town's outskirts, plus a small party detached for the defence of the British Consulate, inconveniently situated in the town centre. Thus, when 2,500 of Kuchik Khan's tribesmen burst out of the forest and into Resht on 20 July they expected to achieve an almost bloodless victory. Instead, their attacks on the camp were ripped apart while those who had surrounded the Consulate were shocked into flight when a Gurkha company, spearheaded by an armoured car, fought its way along the narrow alleys to rescue its embattled occupants. Some of the tribesmen, however, took refuge in buildings from which they sniped whenever an opportunity presented itself. During the next two days the British and Gurkha infantry, supported by the cars, systematically cleared the town of them. They left behind 100 dead and fifty prisoners, some of whom were Austrian. At least an equal number staggered, crawled or were carried back into the trees. Kuchik Khan's reputation as a warlord had gone forever. He was lucky to escape the wrath of his former followers and finally gave himself up, keeping a promise of good behaviour.

When Dunsterville reached Enzeli, he found the local Soviet less truculent than on his former visit. However, when he discovered that they had been conducting an inflammatory correspondence with Kuchik Khan he had the pack of them arrested and sent back to Kasvin. Beyond this, he could only await word of what was taking place in Baku itself. It arrived sooner than he had expected. The Baku Soviet, unable to halt the Turkish advance, had been overthrown and replaced by a body calling itself the Central Caspian Dictatorship. Dunsterville's offer of assistance in defending the town was invoked at once and three steamers, the *President Kruger*, *Kursk* and *Abo*, were placed at his disposal. A small party of Hampshires was sent over at once, accompanied by Major Ruston with four cars (one of which belonged to B Squadron) and some of Duncars' machine-gun teams. Already 39 Infantry Brigade (9th Royal Warwickshire Regiment, 7th Gloucestershire Regiment, 9th Worcestershire Regiment and 7th North Staffordshire Regiment) was moving up from Baghdad and would be shipped across as its various echelons reached Enzeli.

Ruston subsequently recorded his experiences in *Blackwood's Magazine*. Hardly had the troops landed than the former members of the Baku Soviet began fomenting trouble, noisily venting their resentment of the British bourgeoisie's involvement. At one stage it seemed as though fighting would break out between them and the rest of the population. Finally, thanks to the firm attitude of the new arrivals, they were disarmed and warned that if they did not get out of

Astrakhan province immediately, life would become very unpleasant for them. Their leader, a commissar named Petrov, described by Ruston as 'a clever, plausible old scoundrel', was almost incoherent with rage at the prospect of having to explain to his superiors exactly why he had handed over a large quantity of arms and ammunition, plus several batteries of field guns to those whose political views were diametrically opposed to those of the Party.

Peace reigned after the Bolsheviks' departure, but it was of an unwelcome kind. The local troops detailed to defend the town with British assistance were of Armenian origin and made a poor impression on Ruston.

The Armenians, devoid of any sense of duty or discipline and always craven hearted, said: 'Good. The English have come to drive back the Turk. We can go home.' The result of this attitude was that a front of more than ten miles was (for the moment) manned almost entirely by roughly 800 British. The Armenians were well supplied with machine guns and ammunition, though the former were apparently private property for the most part. So-called soldiers would leave the line without permission and go into town on the spree, actually taking their machine guns with them; and, if remonstrated with by their officers (*sic*) would merely shrug their shoulders and retort that they could do as they liked with their own property. Women flitted about the line everywhere. Soldiers, sailors and civilians lazed about in the sun, occasionally firing their rifles in the blue in much the same way as one scares birds. The Chief of local Staff is known to the British as the Village Idiot and lived up to his name.

On 11 August a joint attack was mounted on the village of Mastagi, which was now in Turkish hands. From the garrison's point of view its possession was a matter of some importance as it was from this area that Baku drew its supplies of fruit, vegetables, farm produce and much of its fresh water. It was well suited for defence as it was well-wooded and possessed many stone-walled gardens and outhouses on its outskirts. These had been turned into machine-gun posts by the enemy and were difficult to spot. The area between the Baku garrison's defences and Mastagi was broken and contained excellent cover for snipers. In addition, the minarets of numerous mosques provided the Turks with panoramic observation.

The attack itself was delivered by two Armenian battalions, seventy mounted Cossacks, two armoured cars and four Fords fitted with machine guns, supported by a battery of field guns. The attack was intended to be secret but in this part of the world such things barely existed. The Turks were ready and waiting, so that while the cars and the cavalry performed useful work the infantry made no headway at all. It says much for the accuracy of the Turkish fire that two of the cars' gunners were hit by rounds entering their machine-gun ports. One was killed but the other, despite a painful nose wound, remained in action for the duration of the fighting. One result of the attack's failure was that during the next fortnight food prices in Baku began to rise steeply although, oddly, caviar remained plentiful. However, Colonel Crawford was appointed food controller and not only succeeded in procuring adequate supplies but also set up a distribution system. Some reinforcement came in from Enzeli, and Bicherakov sent down some of his men from his operations against Petrovsk.

The Turks mounted a major offensive on 26 August, beginning with a barrage the intensity and accuracy of which surprised everyone. Their objectives were the village and railway junction of Balajari and the oilfields surrounding it – Griazni Vulkan (known to the British as the Mud Volcano), Binagadi and Balakhani. Their infantry were clearly well trained, disciplined and equipped and came on despite gaps being shot in their ranks. One Armenian battalion bolted at the first shot. Another would have done likewise if their British officer had not shot the ringleader in the leg and threatened the rest with his revolver. There were, however, no barbed-wire defences and at length Ruston's position was swamped. A brief but savage hand-to-hand struggle took place, so intense that he could remember little about it. Having held on for three hours, he and his survivors retreated 400 yards to another position, out of which they were quickly shelled, finally retiring to a position in front of Balajari. It seemed that the Turks had been seriously hurt, for a counter-attack with the bayonet by a company of North Staffords threw them out of most of their gains.

Sergeant Frank Round's Austin was working on the left of the North Staffords, covering their final withdrawal. At this critical moment the interior of the car was filled by the smell of burned-out clutch lining and the vehicle slowed down. Old hands by now, Round and his fellow gunner knew that if it was allowed to stop they would never get it moving again. They jumped out and heaved with all their might while Turkish bullets clanged off the armour. The driver, having unbolted the clutch housing, tossed them his cap and told them to fill it with sandy soil. The clutch plates were then separated and the contents poured between them, providing just sufficient friction for the car to be reversed the 400 yards to safety. The men's actions had been cool and professional and, by some miracle, not one of them had been hit. For others, the position was less happy. British casualties had also been heavy and there were no stretchers on which the worst cases could be carried to the dressing station, which was two miles away. Those of the walking wounded who could were able to get there, where Surgeon Major Scott was working almost single-handed and continued to do so throughout the siege. Ruston remained convinced that the more serious cases, unable to move, were bayoneted by the Turks when they overran the first position.

To Ruston's disgust, the Village Idiot took no steps to strengthen the new positions and continued to rely on a relative handful of British troops, ravaged by dysentery, malaria and influenza, to hold the line against two Turkish divisions. Fortunately, no further action took place until the middle of September when a Turkish officer deserted. He was an Arab and therefore despised by the Turks. Now, tired of their insults, he felt no qualms about disclosing their plans for the next attack. They now possessed 7,000 good quality regulars, supported by Kurdish, Tartar and Georgian irregulars. He also disclosed that they greatly over-estimated the size of the Baku garrison and the date of the coming attack.

At first light on 14 September, exactly as the deserter had predicted, the Turks mounted their carefully planned offensive. They more or less walked over the Armenian positions, leaving a North Staffordshire company isolated on the coastal sector, and pressed on to the garrison's last line of defence.

So far the Turk was top dog [wrote Major Ruston] and to prevent reinforcements coming up, he started demonstrations and side shows all along the line. The battle raged the entire day with alternating success. Those sectors held by the British on the whole remained in our hands; but though the Armenians, scared by the knowledge that they had at last got their backs to the wall, put up a better fight, the mischief was done. The main line had been given up without a struggle, and a second formed line, protected by barbed wire, did not exist. The opening fighting considerably favoured the well-disciplined troops of the enemy. In vain British reinforcements were sent to where the fighting was thickest; they fought like heroes and inflicted heavy losses on the Turks. The company cut off on the coast hacked their way through and, under able leadership, joined in the fray around the cemetery. Armoured cars darted hither and thither, spitting death at the advancing enemy. Many deeds of valour were performed but by six o'clock in the evening the Turks were on the outskirts of the town.

Naturally, this turn of events had been foreseen by Dunsterville and he was not prepared to hazard any more of his men's lives on behalf of people who declined to defend themselves. In preparation for a rapid evacuation he had asked Sergeant Round to set up a machine gun aboard his headquarters ship, the *President Kruger*, to cover the final stages of this. On the morning of the 14th the wounded had been taken aboard the *Kursk* and the *Abo*, which sailed for Enzeli early that evening. When dusk put an end to the fighting in the suburbs he informed the Central Caspian Dictatorship that he was withdrawing his troops that night. The Dictators blustered that their guard–ship would blow the *President Kruger* apart but he ignored them. After dark the exhausted rifle companies began filing their way down to the harbour, sniped at occasionally by their former comrades. The armoured cars were driven onto the pier, rendered useless, and pushed into deep water while the transport echelon was wrecked. The munitions stored in the arsenal were loaded onto a small coaster, the *Armenian*. At 23.00 both vessels sailed. The guard–ship opened fire on them, missed the *President Kruger* altogether but hit the *Armenian* seven times without causing serious damage, despite the tons of explosive stowed aboard. Both ships reached Enzeli the following day while Bicherakov's men returned safely to Debent in their own steamer.

As Dunsterville had been forced to abandon Baku, a superficial view was that he had failed in a mission that few thought had any chance of succeeding. In fact, he had succeeded, for not one drop of priceless Caspian oil reached the Central Powers before Turkey surrendered on 31 October. The surrender terms required them to evacuate the town, which they were in process of doing when 39 Infantry Brigade arrived to take possession. The Turks told them that the siege had cost them 2,000 casualties. British losses during the same period amounted to seventy-one killed and eighty-five wounded, of whom twenty-one died in hospital.

Duncars' personnel returned to Baghdad by easy stages, then travelled downriver to embark on the troopship that would take them on the first stage of their journey home, no doubt reflecting that the Dunsterforce episode had cost them more casualties than they had sustained during the entire time they had served in Russia under Locker Lampson. They reached Southampton on 28 February 1919, many still wearing their light tropical uniforms, and were sent immediately to Belton Park Camp where there were neither huts, heating, blankets nor food waiting for them. Consequently, they were forced to sleep rough in freezing temperatures. A furious, desk-thumping visit by Major Sholl to the War Office secured them accommodation next morning, followed by early release and the right to wear Russian medals, but the damage had been done. Six men died of pneumonia and, among the numerous frostbite cases, one man had a leg amputated and others lost fingers. The administration of the camp was subjected to an immediate inquiry.

As for their remaining armoured cars, they were handed over to 7th LAMB and remained in Mesopotamia until June 1919, when the unit is believed to have been disbanded and the cars sent to India.

Chapter 10

It All Came Tumbling Down

As mentioned in an earlier chapter, the Ottoman Empire's declaration of war against Great Britain, France and Imperial Russia indicated that some kind of Turkish initiative against the Suez Canal could be regarded as inevitable. What was planned in Constantinople, however, amounted to little more than a large-scale raid that would cause damage to installations and possibly block the waterway with sunken ships. The detailed planning was vague as far as designated objectives were set and the possibility that Allied warships had been integrated into the Canal defences was not seriously considered.

The troops detailed for the operation belonged to Djemal Pasha's VIII Corps and were accompanied by a team of German advisers under Freiherr Kress von Kressenstein. By the middle of January 1915 the corps was ready to leave its base at Beersheba and embark on its crossing of the Sinai Desert, from which the British had withdrawn during the previous autumn. It was decided to ignore the easier coastal route as this would have brought its marching columns within range of naval gunfire. The inland route, though hot and arid in summer, was now quite passable as the heavy rains of winter had filled pools and cisterns along the way. Despite this, 5,000 water-carrying camels were still required to prevent thirst becoming an acute problem. Djemal's progress was regularly reported to the British by Nieuport seaplanes flying off the Canal, ensuring that the element of surprise did not exist. When the Turks launched a series of unco-ordinated attacks along a wide front these were defeated in detail and sustained some 2,000 casualties, forcing Djemal to withdraw slowly to Beersheba.

Partly because of a wave of anti-British feeling sweeping across Egypt, partly because the country's British garrison was reduced by the demands of the Gallipoli campaign, and partly because the end of the year saw an outbreak of a frontier war with the Senussi sect across the border in Libya, the course of which has been described in an earlier chapter, the war in the Middle East seemed to be going nowhere. That was certainly the opinion of Lord Kitchener who bluntly asked Lieutenant General Sir Archibald Murray, commander of the Egyptian Expeditionary Force, 'Are you defending the Canal or is it defending you?' In fairness, until Gallipoli was evacuated in December 1915, Murray lacked the resources to expand the war into the Sinai peninsula. After that, with greatly increased manpower resources at his disposal, he was able to act decisively. He reached the conclusion that a renewed Turkish offensive would enter Sinai through El Arish or El Kusseima and decided to establish a fifty-mile front between these two points. First, he set about creating a sound logistic infrastructure. Thousands of local labourers were engaged in constructing a standard-gauge railway from El Kantara on the Canal. The railhead of this advanced across the Sinai at the rate of fifty miles per month, in parallel with a freshwater pipeline complete with storage tanks, a portable reservoir capable of holding 500,000 gallons, and batteries of standpipes. Beyond the railhead an efficient camel transport corps supplied the forward troops.

As well as marching infantry divisions supported by horse-drawn Royal Field Artillery batteries armed with 18-pounder guns, Murray's army contained a high percentage of mounted troops, including Australian Light Horse and New Zealand Mounted Rifle regiments, British Yeomanry regiments, a regiment of French *Chasseurs d'Afrique*, and a Camel Corps. These troops were formed into a Desert Mounted Corps under Lieutenant General Harry Chauvel. Each division contained three mounted brigades, each of three regiments, and a Royal Horse Artillery battery with twelve 13-pounder guns. Some divisions possessed their own organic Light Car Patrol and one or more LAMBs might be attached for specific missions.

Kressenstein was fully aware of what was taking place in Sinai and decided to mount a spoiling attack on Murray's railhead at Romani employing some 18,000 troops, mainly good quality Anatolians and Gallipoli veterans. His own progress was regularly reported and when he launched his attack on 3 August he found that the British were waiting for him. After the 52nd (Lowland) Division had blunted his assault on the coastal sector, Chauvel's mounted brigades closed in to counter-attack from the south. The battle was hardfought but after the Turks had been driven off a vital ridge the heart went out of them and they began to surrender in large numbers. Kressenstein managed to execute a difficult disengagement but the fact remained that the Romani venture had been a complete disaster, costing 5,000 men killed or wounded and a further 4,000 captured. Total British casualties amounted to a little over 1,000.

At El Arish the Turks, worried by the possibility that a land assault might be supported by a naval bombardment, abandoned the town without a fight. Murray pushed on to Rafaw here his opponents made a stand. Many men on both sides had already fought at Gallipoli and the contest was severe. It was at this point that fighting vehicles were employed in the campaign for the first time. The 7th Light Car Patrol, an Australian unit commanded by Lieutenant W. H. P. McKenzie, was ordered into the fight. McKenzie did not dismount his Lewis guns. His Fords bounced across rough going to reach the Rafa road, along which they raced to reach a small depression from which the concentrated fire of his guns broke up a determined attack on the British left. Fighting lasted until 17.00 when, just as the British were preparing to break contact, the 1,600-strong Turkish garrison surrendered; the British losses amounted to 487 men killed, wounded or missing. During the night McKenzie's cars helped evacuate the wounded to the dressing stations and the following morning escorted a party picking up the enemy's abandoned rifles and machine guns.

Murray waited until his railhead caught up with him and then attacked Gaza on 26 March 1917. His objective covered a low hill approximately two miles from the sea. It was dominated from the east by Ali el Muntar ridge and from the south by three further ridges, from east to west the Sheikh Abbas, the Burjabye and the Es Sire. The ground was broken up by fig and olive orchards separated by huge cactus hedges. Because of the natural protection afforded by these the 3,500 men of the Turkish garrison had done very little to fortify the town. Murray's plan involved the 53rd (Welsh) and 54th (East Anglian) Divisions making a conventional advance while the ANZAC Mounted Division swung round the eastern end of Sheikh Abbas Ridge and advanced north in a wide flanking movement to enter Gaza from the north and north-east, taking the Ali el Muntar Ridge in the process. Simultaneously, the Camel Corps and other mounted units would screen the operation against Turkish interference from the east.

Despite ferocious hand-to-hand fighting all went according to plan. By dusk the 53rd Division had linked up with the ANZACs on Ali el Muntar and were looking down into the defenceless streets of Gaza. Then, without the slightest warning, positive orders to withdraw were received. Time and again officers requested confirmation, which they received. As the withdrawal began the Turks, unable to believe their luck, swarmed to the attack, pushing the British back to the line of the Wadi Ghazze. McKenzie's 7th Light Car Patrol, unable to understand what was going on, came across 3 Light Horse Brigade in the process of retiring. The brigade was being closely pursued by the Turks and its commander asked McKenzie to cover its withdrawal. He deployed his five guns along a ridge with their barrels just clearing the crest. They remained silent until the Turks were some 1,500 yards distant, when the order to fire was given. The enemy was cut down in large numbers yet, believing that they were on the point of achieving a great victory, continued to come on. McKenzie retired to the next ridge, and then the next, treating the enemy to a storm of bullets from each that ensured the light horsemen were pulling clear of their pursuers. Finally, at the reformed British line, the Turks were halted and reluctantly turned away.

The disaster cost the British and ANZAC troops 523 killed, 2,932 wounded and 412 missing. The Turkish losses amounted to 301 killed, 1,085 wounded and 1,061 missing. The reason for the debacle was that the two senior officers responsible, Lieutenant General Sir Charles Dobell in overall command and Lieutenant General Sir Philip Chetwode in charge of the flanking attack, had set up a joint command post fifteen miles from Ali el Muntar. Obviously, they had not the slightest idea what was happening, but they reached a joint decision that if Gaza had not been physically captured by sunset the troops should disengage and withdraw. Ironically, while the withdrawal order was being issued, the German officer commanding the Gaza garrison, a Major Tiller, was advising Kressenstein by telephone that his position was desperate and that if further pressure was applied he would have to negotiate a surrender. This transmission was picked up in Cairo as it took place yet, incredibly, despite being of critical importance, its details were not relayed to Dobel until midnight.

Unwisely, Murray reported a success if not quite a victory and exaggerated the Turkish losses. His congratulatory telegrams included one from the King and virtually committed him to a second assault on Gaza. Yet it must have occurred to many that, having come so close to defeat, Kressenstein would take steps to ensure that a similar situation did not arise. A full trench system was dug to the south of the town among the orchards and cactus hedges, while along the road to Beersheba a series of redoubts with interlocking fields of fire was constructed, thereby preventing the sort of mounted flank attack that had come so close to succeeding on 26 March. Finally, Beersheba itself was fortified..

Murray's options were therefore limited to a frontal assault, which he rashly entrusted to Dobell. This would be delivered in line with the 54th Division on the right, 52nd Division in the centre and 53rd Division on the left. A detachment of tanks was also present and, to satisfy each of his divisional commanders' importunate demands that it should be attached to their own division, Dobell divided it between them, despite the fact that this ran quite contrary to the tank commander's recommendation that the best results could only be produced if they were employed en masse.

The Second Battle of Gaza commenced on 17 April. The tanks achieved isolated successes but half were lost from one cause or another. The infantry found itself fighting in conditions that resembled those on the Western Front, their casualties amounting to 509 killed, 4,539 wounded and 1,576 missing for little or no gain. The Turks lost 402 men killed, 1,364 wounded and 245 missing. Murray dismissed Dobell but on 11 June was himself informed that he was to be relieved. It was a sad ending for a capable, intelligent officer who had brought his army across the Sinai in good order, yet while he was not personally involved in the two most recent disastrous battles the truth was that he bore the ultimate responsibility.

His successor was General Sir Edmund Allenby, a former Inspector General of Cavalry who had commanded the Cavalry Corps during the First Battle of Ypres and later the Third Army. Nicknamed The Bull because of his furious bellowing when angry, he promptly removed his General Headquarters from the fleshpots of Cairo to a more spartan location just behind the lines at Rafa as this enabled him to exercise immediate forward control and at the same time become a familiar figure to the troops. His most important task, however, was to restore the dented morale of his army and in this respect several months would be required before it could be considered ready to tackle the defences of the Gaza-Beersheba Line.

Despite this, the Turks had no reason to feel that they had brought the overall situation in this theatre of the war under control. In Arabia the rule of Constantinople, a curious mixture of indifference, contempt and cruelty, was detested by the indigenous Arab tribes. In the early summer of 1916 the Sherif of Mecca, Sheikh Hussein, had proclaimed a rebellion in which his son Feisal would act as his field commander. Mecca fell into the rebels' hands quickly but the Turkish garrison of Medina, commanded by one Fakhri Pasha, a murderous old scoundrel with an iron grip on his men, continued to hold out as its possession was considered to be essential to the preservation of national prestige. That those in Constantinople should consider that such a course of action was possible stemmed from the existence of the Hejaz or Pilgrim railway which had been completed shortly before the war and ran all the way from Damascus in Syria and down the Arabian peninsula to Medina itself. It was a remarkable engineering achievement and actually made a profit during its short years of commercial activity, as the journey took just three days as opposed to several weeks in a camel caravan that was vulnerable to the demands of local tribes. Even when completed the tribes were inclined to plunder its materials for their own uses and for this reason the majority of its stations were actually blockhouses containing a unit of soldiers, plus a workshop, water and fuel supplies for locomotives and triangles on which they could be turned around.

It was immediately apparent to the British that the Arab revolt could be most thoroughly exploited by mounting attacks against the Hejaz railway, derailing its trains and damaging its engineering assets such as bridges and culverts. The idea was not to render the line permanently unusable but to make the Turks deploy men and materials to guard and repair it, for troops deployed into distant Arabia could not be employed in Palestine. The British willingly supplied gold, weapons and advisers, of whom the best known was Captain (later Colonel) T. E. Lawrence, a professional archaeologist who spoke fluent Arabic and who supported the cause of Arab unity. He is sometimes portrayed as a dreamer whose eyes were focused on distant horizons, yet the truth was that he was also a practical man who, while understanding the potential of modern weapons, appreciated the limitations of the irregulars who formed the greater part of the Arab army. They fought the Turk for pleasure and plunder and would leave the army for long periods to enjoy the latter. Among others, Lawrence persuaded Feisal that the chances of success would be considerably improved if he created a regular army capable of remaining together between operations.

Unable to take Medina, Feisal's small but expanding force of rebels began moving north along the Red Sea coast and in December 1916 captured the port of Wejh, which became its base and the route by which, for the moment, the Royal Navy was able to keep it supplied with weapons and ammunition. Yet, perversely, it was while leading a force of Bedouin irregulars that Lawrence achieved his first major success, storming the fortified port of Aqaba, at the head of the gulf of the same name, in a dashing attack from the landward side. The incident ensured that from now on both Lawrence and the Arabs would be taken seriously. During a personal meeting between Lawrence and Allenby it was agreed that the Arab forces would be given the definite role of protecting Allenby's right flank when he finally advanced into Palestine.

In addition to the defences already existing at the stations and depots along the Hejaz line, the Turks had begun protecting their trains with flat cars on which machine guns and even artillery weapons were mounted within the protection accorded by layers of sandbags, plus an unknown number of riflemen including reinforcements and units on posting. An attack by unsupported Arab horsemen was, therefore, extremely dangerous, even if a train was derailed or trapped between sections of track destroyed by demolition charges. At the very least, mobile heavy weapons were required to neutralise those carried by the trains. Because of this the Hejaz Armoured Car Section of two Rolls Royce cars was formed in May 1917 under Captain Gilman, its designation being changed to battery in December of that year when it was joined by two more Rolls Royces. Also serving with Lawrence from August 1917 onwards was No. 10 Section Royal Field Artillery consisting of six Talbot lorries, two of which were armed with 10-pounder mountain guns while the third was fitted with a Maxim pom-pom; the remainder carried ammunition and spare parts. The transport echelon for the mechanised units consisted of five Rolls Royces with box bodies and six box-body Fords armed with Lewis guns that were identical to those used by the light car patrols save that they were fitted with special wheels permitting the use of oversize tyres which helped considerably in areas of deep sand. The men manning the vehicles of the various sub-units were drawn from various parts of the Army; the crews of the Rolls Royce armoured cars belonged to the Machine Gun Corps, the Talbots were manned by the Royal Field Artillery under the command of Lieutenant Brodie although their drivers and fitters had been seconded from the Army Service Corps.

Once Allenby's build-up was complete, his plan for breaking the Gaza-Beersheba Line involved taking the latter and its all-important wells by *coup de main* while a major diversionary attack on Gaza occupied the Turks' attention. Only Chauvel's Desert Mounted Corps was considered to possess the necessary speed and punch to execute the Beersheba end of the operation before the Turks could destroy the wells. It was to carry out a long approach march through the desert and then launch an immediate attack on the town from the east and south-east while XX Corps, with four infantry divisions, mounted holding attacks on the Turkish line to the west and XXI Corps, with three infantry divisions, would carry out the feint attack on Gaza itself.

The Third Battle of Gaza commenced on 31 October. Emerging unexpectedly out of the desert the ANZAC and Australian Mounted Divisions were forced to overcome stiff resistance from the outposts of the 5,000-strong Beersheba garrison, but a thundering charge by 4 Light Horse Brigade swept over two lines of trenches and on into Beersheba itself where most of the vital wells were captured intact and the enemy threw down their arms. So great had been the shock engendered by the dashing attack of Chauvel's troopers that the shaken Turks had forgotten to lower the sights on their rifles, the result being that most of their fire went high. Those Turkish formations to the west of Beersheba, their flank now turned, were forced to retreat under continuous pressure from XX Corps.

The real surprise of the day, however, was the collapse of Turkish resistance at Gaza itself. There XXI Corps had digested the unfortunate lessons of the Second Battle of Gaza. The Tank Detachment had been brought up to strength by the delivery of Mark IV tanks and had been placed under the command of a single division, the 54th, which would attack on frontage of 5,000 yards during the night of 1/2 November. Working closely together, infantry and tanks carved their way through the defences and by dawn had broken out into open country. That this was the correct method of employment for tanks was confirmed by the detachment's total casualties during the battle – just one killed and two wounded.

The Turks attempted to stand at Huj on 8 November and again at El Maghar five days later, but on both occasions determined attacks by British Yeomanry regiments drove them off their positions, albeit at some cost in men and horses. On 14 November two Rolls Royce armoured cars belonging to 12th LAMB broke into Junction Station, where the Jerusalem branch left the main line, to find a Turkish battalion carrying out demolition tasks. Opening fire, the cars chased them out of the station and for two miles beyond, less than half the scattered fugitives being able to make good their escape. The direct pursuit ended with the capture of Jaffa by the ANZAC Mounted Division on 16 November. Most of the subsequent fighting took place in the Judean hills where the Turks were able to slow down the British advance but not halt it. During the morning of 9 December the last Turkish garrison marched out of Jerusalem and later that day the first British troops entered the city by the Jaffa Gate. Allenby's 1917 offensive had cost 18,000 British casualties, but the Turks had lost 25,000 men and their morale was seriously shaken.

Kressenstein lost his job and was replaced by General Erich von Falkenhayn, a former Chief of General Staff of the German Army. When the Gaza-Beersheba Line collapsed Falkenhayn had commanded a force of fourteen divisions and the 6,000-strong German Asia Corps, known collectively as the *Yilderim* (Lightning) Army Group. This had originally been formed with the object of recovering Baghdad, but in Falkenhayn's view the Palestine front held more potential dangers than did Mesopotamia and it was to Palestine that it was now directed. Nevertheless, because of the leisurely manner in which Yilderim conducted its affairs, its German advisers considered the title to be the most infuriatingly inaccurate of misnomers, especially as it had failed to reach Jerusalem before it was abandoned, although in the subsequent fighting to the north it had managed to establish a coherent front. Further operations were hindered by the heaviest rains in living memory and finally the opposing lines settled down to stretch between the sea and the Jordan valley.

Whatever plans Allenby might have had for the spring of 1918 had to be abandoned as he was forced to strip his command of troops who were urgently needed in France to counter the extremely dangerous Ludendorff series of offensives. He did, however, discuss and plan with Lawrence a number of mechanised operations designed to ensure the security of Feisal's army against attacks from the south as well as preparatory measures enabling that army to cover the British right when the advance to the north was resumed. He was anxious that the enemy garrisons at Ma'an and Es Salt should be eliminated by the Arab irregulars while the armoured cars and Talbot lorries under Major Alan Dawnay took Shahm and Mudowiara and inflicted permanent damage on the railway between the two, the intention being that the garrison of Medina and those Turkish units holding posts along the railway's southern section, a total of 12,000 men, should be isolated and prevented from interfering with events in Palestine and Syria.

Lawrence, the irregular *par excellence*, was troubled that Dawnay, a regular officer, was leading armoured cars on a raid for the first time. On the night before the raid he visited Dawnay and went over the latter's plans with him and found that they could not be faulted either as to method or timings. At dawn the cars, idling their way forward in almost total silence, arrived among the Turkish outposts without the need to fire a shot and received the surrender of their astonished occupants. This cleared the way for Captain Hornby with two Rolls Royce tenders laden with explosives, to blow up the nearest bridge. Inexperienced in such matters, Hornby employed enough explosives to destroy a small town. Lawrence rode over to demonstrate the less expensive methods of destruction he had learned over recent months and the two spent the rest of the day destroying bridges and sections of the line so efficiently that they were beyond immediate repair. Next, the Talbots opened fire on a stone blockhouse with their mountain guns and pom-poms, providing cover for the Arabs to close in and effect the capture of the post. By now the Arabs had thoroughly warmed to their work. Supported once more by the Talbots, now joined by the armoured cars and two British aircraft, they closed in on Shahm station and were on the point of making their final assault when the Turks surrendered, ten minutes earlier than had been expected, according to Dawnay's timetable. The Arabs were permitted to loot the station and its storehouse, led by Lawrence who had taken a fancy to the station bell. The following day the cars took Ramleh station, which was found to be unoccupied, but on the third day of the operation the cars attacked Mudowwara station but were not supported by the Egyptian element of the column and were forced to retire. Elsewhere, Feisal's regulars, unable to make progress against the defences of Es Salt and Ma'an, were also forced to withdraw, although the overall objective of the operation had been achieved because of extensive demolitions along the undefended portions of the railway which resulted in the eighty-mile stretch of the line between Ma'an and Mudowwara being wrecked beyond any prospect of repair. Despite this, the Turks were marginally encouraged by their defence of Ma'an and made a sortie against Aba el Lissan, Feisal's advance base. Laurence, informed of this, despatched the cars which inflicted such losses on the attackers that never again did they leave the safety of their blockhouses and trenches.

Once the danger posed by Ludendorff's offensives on the Western Front had passed, it became possible to rebuild Allenby's strength with replacements from India. His intention was to strike a decisive blow on the coastal sector of the front, but every effort was made to convince the Turks that it would be made in the valley of the river Jordan. A broadly-based deception plan involved the construction of dummy camps made from old, worn tents, dummy gun parks and battery positions built from old wheels, pipes and logs and dummy horses made from wood frames, blankets and canvas assembled into formal horse lines suggesting that the whole Desert Mounted Corps was present. There was also constant bustle accompanied by dust clouds generated by mule-drawn sledges and camp fires galore at dusk. Behind the sector chosen for the real attack troops moved by night into concealed bivouacs among the orange groves or into camps the size of which had been increased two months earlier. No fires were permitted and all cooking was carried out using smokeless solidified alcohol.

Allenby's intention was to destroy the Turkish army at a stroke. An infantry breakthrough on the coastal sector would be exploited with a huge wheel to the right by the Desert Mounted Corps, severing the Turks' communications as it carved its way to the Jordan valley. The breakthrough itself would be made by Lieutenant General Sir Edward Bulfin's XXI Corps, deploying from the right, the 54th, 3rd Indian, 75th, 7th Indian and 60th Divisions, plus a small French contingent, along a fifteen-mile sector close to the coast. The subsequent exploitation would be carried out by the Desert Mounted Corps (the 4th and 5th Cavalry Divisions and the Australian Mounted Division) through the gains made by XXI Corps. Holding the remaining forty-five miles of front were XX Corps' 10th and 53rd Divisions plus the troops in the Jordan valley. Allenby's artillery was flexibly handled and achieved an overwhelming concentration of force on the planned breakthrough sector.

Across the lines Falkenhayn had been replaced by General Liman von Sanders, head of the German Military Mission and successful defender of the Gallipoli peninsula. His experience there had convinced him that ground must be held whatever the cost, although the fact was that ground was of far less value here than it was in the Dardanelles. Under his command were three armies, which in reality were simply over-large corps. From the sea Djevad Pasha's Eighth Army held a twenty-mile front extending to Furqa. From Furqa to the Jordan valley the front was held by the Seventh Army under Mustapha Kemal, another Gallipoli veteran. The Trans-Jordan and desert flank was held by Djemal Kucuk's Fourth Army, which included the German 146th Regiment. In immediate reserve were units containing some 3,000 men. Liman von Sanders' General Headquarters was located at Nazareth, rather too far behind the front but to connected to Eighth Army Headquarters at Tul Karm and Seventh Army Headquarters at Nablus by means of telephone lines that ran through a main switchboard in Afula.

To sum up, Allenby's army was the larger and more modern in equipment and outlook. It consisted of 11,000 cavalry, 56,000 infantry, 552 guns, and had become familiar with mechanised operations involving fighting vehicles, contained an efficient air element and was supported by a modern logistic and signals' infrastructure. Liman von Sanders' army, on the other hand, consisted of 3,000 cavalry, 32,000 infantry and 370 guns. It relied to a greater degree on animal rather than mechanised transport and fighting vehicles were rarely employed. Its logistic support depended on a rickety railway system. It possessed a small air element although this lacked the capacity for anything other than local intervention. Worst of all, Allenby's plans envisaged a mobile battle with strategic aims, whereas the best that Liman von Sanders could expect was to retain the status quo. However, that seemed unlikely for a number of reasons. First, neither the number of his guns and machine guns per mile of front, nor the width of his wire, nor the overall depth of his defences came close to that of the Western Front and these factors in themselves enhanced the possibility of a breakthrough. Secondly, so much of his hinterland consisted of good cavalry country in which the Desert Mounted Corps could be used to good effect.

The Battle of Megiddo, named after the battle fought in 1469 BC over much the same ground, began during the night of 18/19 September. XX Corps mounted a diversionary attack designed to convince the Turks that the main assault was to be delivered in the Jordan Valley and, shortly after midnight, the RAF became active, raiding the headquarters of the Turkish Seventh and Eighth Armies as well as Afula, where the main military telephone exchange was wrecked along with Eighth Army's radio stations, the result being that Liman von Sanders would begin the battle without contact with and therefore effective control of his troops. Elsewhere, the usual patrol activity took place in no man's land, although the infantrymen of XXI Corps were silently leaving their trenches and moving up to their start lines, indicated by previously laid white tapes. At 04.50 the British bombardment, the heaviest ever fired in this theatre of war, thundered out. At times no less than 1,000 shells per minute were exploding in the enemy's lines, from which SOS rockets soared skywards. The Turkish artillery replied at once but most of its counter bombardment landed in the recently vacated trenches.

The British and Indian infantry came on very quickly. The enemy's thin belt of barbed wire was soon breached with planks, corrugated iron and stuffed sandbags. A volley of grenades burst along the parapets and then the attackers went in with the bayonet. Most of the defenders were too stunned to offer resistance. Mass surrenders took place immediately, then the artillery switched to firing a rolling barrage behind which the follow-up waves of attackers pushed ever deeper into the Turkish rear areas. The advance spread along the length of XXI Corps' frontage which was beginning to swing to the east like the opening of a gate. Through that gate streamed the Desert Mounted Corps with the 4th Cavalry Division on the right and the 5th Cavalry Division on the left. The task of the former, with the 11th LAMB and the 1st Light Car Patrol attached, was to secure the Musmus Pass through the Carmel Range and cut the railway near Afula. A detachment was then to be sent to seize the bridges over the Jordan and Yarmuk at Jisr el Majami while the main body advanced on Beisan. On the coast naval gunfire support had eased the passage of the 5th Cavalry Division, with 12th LAMB and 7th LCP attached.

With his ground communications destroyed, Liman von Sanders was groping in the fog of war and had not the slightest idea what was going on. Nor was his air arm able to help as the RAF was sitting on top of his airfields, making take-off impossible. He did, however, appreciate the critical importance of the Musmus Pass and managed to scrape together the equivalent of six infantry companies under the command of a Major Frey, an engineer officer, to guard the northern exit from the pass. Why he chose to defend this is a mystery as the summit of the pass was a far more difficult obstacle for an attacker to take. Be that as it may, the chilly dawn of 21 September found Frey's advance guard singing and warming themselves around their fires when through thinning darkness came the 2nd Lancers from the head of the pass, lances lowered to the engage, accompanied by two of 11th LAMB's armoured cars. Such was the Turks' surprise that they surrendered immediately.

Having watered his horses, the Lancers' commander, Captain W. S. Davison, received orders to proceed to Afula. Expecting trouble, he continued his advance with three squadrons in line. At 05.30 the regiment came under fire from a considerable Turkish force deployed in front of the village of Birket el Fuleh. Davison immediately formed a fire base with the regiment's own machine-gun teams, the armoured cars and centre squadron while the rest of the regiment took advantage of dead ground to conceal its approach to a position from which it charged the enemy's left. The entire engagement lasted five minutes at the end of which forty-six Turks had been speared and 470 captured. The enemy had been the main body of the force intended to hold the Musmus Pass. Its commander, Major Frey, had left the scene before the charge was delivered. The lancers' casualties amounted to one man wounded and twelve horses killed.

Resuming its advance, the regiment reached Afula at 07.45 and immediately came under fire. This quickly spluttered into silence when the Deccan Horse, belonging to the 5th Cavalry Division, was also developing an attack on the town. By 08.00 the garrison, consisting of seventy-five Germans and 200 Turks, had ceased firing and given themselves up. Useful booty captured at the railway station were ten locomotives and fifty trucks, a large stock of petrol, a supply of champagne and three aircraft, a fourth carrying mail being shot down as it attempted to land. A convoy of twelve German lorries, attempting to escape along the Beisan road, was run down by the armoured cars.

On the same night that the Musmus Pass was captured a detachment of 5th Cavalry Division was despatched to Nazareth in the hope of capturing Liman von Sanders' General Headquarters and, if possible, the general himself. The Gloucestershire Yeomanry might well have achieved the latter had it not been for the defence put up by his Staff and GHQ clerks, who also managed to burn their classified papers. According to his housekeeper, Liman von Sanders made a pyjama–clad escape in his car and managed to form a temporary GHQ at Samakh at the southern end of Lake Tiberias.

By now, the overall situation was that a major portion of the Desert Mounted Corps was advancing eastwards across the communications of the Turkish Eighth and Seventh Armies while, simultaneously, those same armies were under maintained pressure from the British XXI and XX Corps to the south. Frantic staffs issued orders for Turkish units to retire to locations that were already in British hands. Bereft of meaningful orders from above, the majority of Turks gave up rather than fight. The Eighth Army had virtually ceased to exist by sunset of the 20th and its remnants were rapidly disintegrating into a mob of fugitives. A major portion of the Turkish Seventh Army was struggling to conduct an orderly retreat along the Wadi Far'a when it was bounced by the RAF. First, the head of its long column was attacked bringing the remainder to a standstill. Then, throughout the day, two aircraft appeared every three minutes to bomb and strafe, with an additional six aircraft every half-hour. Along a two–mile stretch the road became choked with smashed and abandoned vehicles and guns. Very few of the enemy were found dead amidst the wreckage; most had fled into the hills and were either captured or gave themselves up. It took several days to extract about 100 guns from the tangle, sections of which could only be cleared by burning. This was the first occasion in history when a major formation was wiped out by air power alone.

The only surviving Turkish army was Djevad Pasha's Fourth, east of the Jordan. Fugitives from the broken Eighth and Seventh Armies headed for the known bridges and fords but comparatively few of them got through. Even then, Djevad's army was itself coming under attack from a formation known as Chaytor's Force after its commander, Major General Sir E. W. C. Chaytor, consisting of the ANZAC Mounted Division, 20 Indian Infantry Brigade, several independent infantry battalions and some artillery support, operating east of the Jordan some miles ahead of the point it entered the Dead Sea and was closing in on Amman. Simultaneously, Feisal's Arab army had begun mounting attacks against Djevad's troops from the east. Knowing that he could expect no assistance from the Turkish formations now trapped in Arabia, he took the only course possible and began retreating northwards along the railway to Dera'a and Damascus.

Back in Palestine, the disintegration of Turkish armies continued. On 22 September Allenby arrived at the headquarters of the Desert Mounted Corps in El Lajjun. Chauvel told him that so far he had taken some 15,000 prisoners. 'No bloody good to me!' replied the army commander in the full knowledge that he had destroyed Liman von Sanders' army. 'I want 30,000 from you before you've done!' There seemed to be nothing that could halt the advance, yet, here and there, there were Turkish and German troops who had not been exposed to the battle's first devastating blow and were still willing to fight.

The task of capturing Haifa was given to Brigadier General C. R. Harbord's 15 Cavalry Brigade. The Turkish garrison consisted of a depot regiment, a machine-gun company and some artillery. It had not been touched by the general collapse and was occupying a strong position in that the direct approach to the town lay along a narrow neck of land between the Mount Carmel Ridge to the south and the River Kishon (Nahr el Muqatta) to the north. Harbord mounted a three-pronged attack commencing at 14.00 on 23 September. The leading squadron of Mysore Lancers was engaged by machine guns firing from north of the river and also the northern slopes of Mount Carmel, and by artillery located near a religious establishment, the Karmelheim, at the western end of the ridge. A second squadron, supported by the Sherwood Rangers from 14 Cavalry Brigade, was to follow the track along the summit of Mount Carmel and charge the guns. In the centre the two remaining Mysore squadrons would provide fire support for a charge by the Jodhpore Lancers along the neck of land and into the town.

The Jodhpores had hardly begun their approach when they watched in horror as two of their ground scouts vanished from view in the Kishon quicksands. The leading squadron immediately swung left and charged the machine gunners on Carmel's lower slopes, which it did successfully. This opened the defile for the rest of the regiment to charge into the town along the road and railway, followed by the Mysore fire support squadrons. Up on Mount Carmel itself the Mysore squadron made a difficult ascent, losing horses from exhaustion, lameness and enemy fire, so that when the moment came for the attack only fifteen mounted men remained. These nevertheless executed a charge over broken, stoney ground, supported by two machine guns and the squadron's Hotchkiss section from a flank. They captured a 150mm naval gun, two mountain guns, and seventy-eight prisoners. At this moment the first of the Sherwood Rangers arrived to follow through with the pursuit, and captured a further fifty Turks.

The action could have gone badly wrong but was won by the speed, aggression and professionalism of those involved. Altogether, two naval, four 4.2-inch, six 77mm and four 10-pounder camel guns were taken, as well as ten machine guns, a large quantity of ammunition and stores and numerous – very welcome – fresh horses. Casualties included Lieutenant Colonel Thakur Dalpat Singh, commanding the Jodhpore Lancers, and two others killed, thirty-four wounded, sixty-four horses killed and eighty-three horses wounded. Four days later the first supplies were landed at Haifa.

On 25 September an even fiercer engagement took place at Samakh, which was now the last town in all of Palestine to remain in Turkish hands. Following his escape from Nazareth, Liman von Sanders had not spent long in Samakh before departing for Dera'a but he had let it be known that he intended the town to be the hinge of a new holding line that he was struggling to construct. To that end he had reinforced the garrison with German machine gunners and ordered its commander, Captain von Keyserling, that it must be held to the last man. Shortly before dawn on 25 September Brigadier General W. Grant's 4 Australian Light Horse Brigade, which the previous year had carried out its epic charge at Beersheba, launched an attack on the town. On this occasion, however, the brigade's numbers were seriously depleted, as 4th Australian Light Horse were guarding Chauvel's headquarters and five troops of 12th ALH were escorting the ever-growing columns of prisoners. Grant had been promised reinforcements but rather than wait for these to arrive he had ordered 11th ALH to make a mounted attack across open ground from the south-east, covered by machine-gun fire. The remainder of 12th ALH was held in reserve.

At 04.25 11th ALH, under the command of Lieutenant Colonel J. W. Parsons, charged with drawn swords in two lines of half-squadrons with about 200 yards between lines, yelling so as to indicate their position to the supporting machine gunners. Men and horses started to go down to the enemy's return fire, but the Australians broke through the eastern defences and, sheathing their swords, went in with the rifle and bayonet. As the Australian *Official History* relates:

Dawn came up on one of the hottest and most fiercely contested fights of the whole campaign as the two Australian squadrons assaulted the station buildings. The enemy lined a stout stone wall, fired automatic rifles from the windows, hurled bombs. Several parties had established themselves in engines and tenders in the sidings. The struggle raged for a full hour, quarter being neither asked nor given, until every man of the defenders had been killed or wounded. In the village itself, where a squadron of 12th ALH took part, afterwards moving on for the final stages of the battle for the station, the fighting was less severe and here a number of prisoners were taken. By 05.30 it was all over. Two motor boats lying at the jetty made off in the midst of the action but one was caught by a burst from a Hotchkiss rifle, broke into flames and sank.

About 100 Germans were killed. Among the 364 prisoners taken were some 200 Turks who had played little part in the fighting. One gun, ten machine guns, an aircraft and a quantity of rolling stock were captured. The Australians' casualties amounted to seventy-eight killed and wounded, and they also lost nearly 100 horses, most of which were killed. Grant now ordered one squadron of 12th ALH to move up the western shore of the lake towards Tiberias. In so doing it encountered a squadron of 8th ALH and 12th LAMB and the combined force pushed on to occupy the town against slight opposition, taking nearly 100 prisoners and thirteen machine guns.

Beyond the Jordan, Chaytor's ANZAC Mounted Division continued its advance from Es Salt to Amman, hastened by a message dropped from an aircraft to the effect that the garrison of the latter was pulling out. Its rearguard, however, continued to put up stiff resistance. A mounted attack by the Canterbury Mounted Rifles was temporarily stopped by machine-gun fire from the Citadel, but the regiment dismounted and cleared the position with the bayonet, concurrently with Brigadier General G. de L. Ryrie's 2 Light Horse Brigade over-running a number of sangars and then fighting its way into the town, where resistance collapsed at about 13.30. Captures included 2,563 prisoners, ten guns, numerous machine guns, 300 horses and a large quantity of forage.

In fact, Djemal Kucuk had already delayed the withdrawal of his Fourth Army for too long. Together, Chaytor and Feisal had so wrecked the railway that it was no longer possible to use it south of Dera'a.

Turkish units in that area therefore faced a long, thirsty march with the Arabs always hovering on their flanks, fully aware that the latter would show not the slightest mercy to stragglers and the wounded. Major General Sir George Barrow had already received orders for his 4th Cavalry Division to proceed eastwards beyond the Jordan to Dera'a itself and on the morning of 28 September rode into the town at the head of 10 Cavalry Brigade. At the railway station he was greeted by one of the most horrific sights of the entire war. A long hospital train, full of sick and wounded Turks, lay halted with the driver and his fireman still in their cab, alive but mortally wounded. Arabs were going from carriage to carriage, tearing the clothes off the patients, regardless of their injuries, then cutting their throats. Barrow ordered them to be pitched off the train, which he then placed under British guard. In other respects the incident was notable for a furious meeting between Barrow and Lawrence, each of whom took an instant dislike to the other.

Allenby's declared objective was now Damascus. On 27 September the Australian Mounted Division found the bridge at Jisr Banat Yakub partially demolished and the eastern bank of the Jordan held in force. Heavy fire was exchanged across the river but after dark several fords were discovered, enabling the Australians to cross before dawn. By then, the enemy had broken contact and withdrawn in motor lorries. The Australians filed up the Golan Heights and entered the town of Kuneitra at 13.00 on 28 September. By now a number of horses were showing signs of foundering as a result of the heavy demands made on them during the past week. The 11th LAMB took the lead the following morning and ran into the Turkish rearguard at Sa'sa, deployed across the road on rising ground covered with boulders with additional protection provided by a lava field containing wide crevasses on their left. The enemy had pre-registered his machine-gun fire which remained accurate even after dusk. Nightfall enabled the 9th and 10th ALH to work their way round the Turkish flanks but the going was difficult and it was not until 02.00 that this began to produce results.

The 8th ALH were ordered to make a dismounted attack along the road and by 03.15 the position was in Australian hands. Seven machine guns were captured but, once again, most of the enemy had already made good their escape in motor vehicles.

Later in the day the sound of artillery fire to the east indicated that Barrow's 4th Cavalry Division was forcing the Fourth Army's rearguard to fall back on Damascus. Those of the enemy still opposing Hodgson's Australians were obviously unsettled by these indications and greater numbers of them began to surrender. At Kaukab, just eleven miles from Damascus, a large body of them were found to be holding a strong position, but they took to their heels when Hodgson mounted a full divisional attack. At the same time the 5th Cavalry Division, coming up on the right, intercepted and captured most of a 2,000-strong column at Kiswe.

The fugitive Fourth Army was now streaming through Damascus in two directions, part taking the road to Homs and the north while the remainder headed west through the Barada Gorge towards Riyaq and Beirut. At about 16.30 the Australian Mounted Division, led by the French *Regiment Mixte* and the 2nd New Zealand Machine Gun Squadron, reached the edge of the cliffs overlooking the 100-yard-wide gorge and opened fire on the thousands of troops, transport vehicles and railway trains below. Two miles to the west, the 9th ALH also reached the edge of the gorge and did likewise. Although the enemy fired back, the result was virtually a massacre. Some 400 dead lay sprawled in the road and it took several days to clear the way through the pass. For the moment the city itself remained in Turkish hands but during the evening its military governor, Ali Riza Pasha al Rikabi, arrived at Barrow's headquarters and informed the general that it was not in a defensible state. The following morning, 1 October, the Australians entered Damascus at about the same time as the Arab Army, followed by the 5th Cavalry Division at 10.30. Within the city's barracks several hundred Turks waited passively for their captors to lead them to the prisoner of war cages.

Allenby had achieved an enormous amount. He had ejected the
Turks from Palestine, destroyed three armies, overrun much of Syria
and taken Damascus, and now decided that he would continue his
advance as far as Aleppo. This was easier said than done as, casualties
apart, many of the Desert Mounted Corps' horses had foundered
because of the heavy demands made upon them and been destroyed.
Of the remainder, the artillery was entitled to the first choice for its
gun teams. Just as serious were outbreaks of malaria and influenza,
contracted from the Turks. During the worst week over 3,000 men
were hospitalised and over four times as many deaths stemmed from
these diseases as had been incurred during the battle itself.

The burden of the extended pursuit fell on Macandrew's 5th Cavalry
Division which, albeit the healthiest in the corps, had been reduced
to just 1,500 sabres. Fortunately, additional mechanised units had
now reached the front and Macandrew was given the 2nd, 11th and
12th LAMBS and the 1st, 2nd and 7th Light Car Patrols to act as an
advance guard, as well as being allocated an RAF squadron. Once the
Barada Gorge had been cleared the armoured cars headed for Riyaq,
which was taken without opposition on 6 October. The following day
the cars discovered that the enemy had also abandoned Beirut. Two
days later XXI Corps' composite cavalry regiment and the 7th Indian
Division passed through the city to reach Tripoli on 13 October,
thereby providing Allenby with an additional supply port.

For the long run north Macandrew had reorganised his division
into two columns. Column A consisted of the mechanised units and
15 Cavalry Brigade, and possessed the necessary speed, punch and
firepower for deep penetration. Column B contained the rest of the
division and would go into action as and when needed. In this manner
the division reached Homs on 16 October and continued down the
valley of the Orontes with the Arab army moving along a parallel route
some distance to the east. When Macandrew reached Hama on 20
October Allenby ordered him to halt but changed his mind when the
former convinced him that there was no opposition worth speaking

of left in Aleppo, a fact confirmed by his air squadron's reports of the enemy leaving the city in large numbers. Two days later the advance guard fought a running battle with a Turkish motor convoy protected by an improvised German armoured car. Like most German armoured cars, this was a great lumbering monster that was heavier and slower than its Rolls Royce opponents and was further handicapped by its solid tyres. When two Turkish aircraft appeared those aboard the convoy no doubt viewed them as angels of deliverance and were mortified when they joined in on the side of the British. At this, the German armoured car was hastily abandoned by its crew, who fled.

Saragab was taken on 24 October, but the following day found Column A two days' march ahead of the division's main body, despite which Macandrew sent a car from one of the light car patrols into Aleppo under a flag of truce to demand the city's surrender. The senior Turkish officer present was Mustapha Kemal who rejected the summons. This was pure bluff as he was already preparing to pull out in the face of growing Arab pressure from the east. When Macandrew's armoured cars entered the city on 26 October it was already in Arab hands and 15 Cavalry Brigade was engaging the Turkish rearguard at Haritan. On the 29th Macandrew's division and the Arabs captured Muslimiya Junction through which the enemy's railway lifeline ran into Mesopotamia as well as Palestine. Constantinople requested an armistice, which was granted on 31 October.

In the thirty-eight days that had passed since the start of the Battle of Megiddo, Allenby's troops had advanced 350 miles, taken 76,000 prisoners and captured 360 guns and eighty-nine locomotives; no accurate figures exist for the numbers of Turkish killed and wounded. This victory, as complete as any in history, had been achieved at the cost of only 782 killed, 4,179 wounded and 382 missing. The Ottoman Empire, once the terror of Europe, had lost its provinces in Arabia, Mesopotamia, Palestine and the Levant, and it could no longer claim to be guardian of the holy cities of Mecca, Baghdad and Jerusalem. Like the walls of Jericho those many years gone by, the walls had suddenly come tumbling down.

Chapter 11

Grand Finale

During the later weeks of summer 1918 there was much food for thought both in the opposing Allied and German lines on the Western Front. With difficulty and considerable loss, the British had withstood Ludendorff's series of offensives and, having recovered much of their strength, still believed in eventual victory. This was strengthened by the United States' entry into the war and the arrival of large numbers of American troops in France. Their only reservations on that score were that, for the moment, the Americans were inexperienced, although it was accepted that, given time, that phase would pass, and also the fact that the US Army had expanded to its present size so quickly that it was short of vital equipment, including tanks and artillery, although Allied sources were being employed to remedy these deficiencies.

Across the lines the climate was one of depression. The troops had been promised that the great offensives of the spring would produce victory and, although they had won ground, that promise remained unfulfilled. The elite storm troop battalions, formed from the finest soldiers, had been torn to shreds and, inevitably, the rest of the Army was of lesser quality. Repeated bloodbaths, including the Somme, Verdun and Passchendaele, had almost destroyed its junior leadership. The vital strata provided by the career NCOs had maintained the Army's backbone but had been thinned too often, as had the professional officer corps. The latter, unwilling to diminish their privileged position in German society, refused to grant temporary commissions and instead began granting the condescending title of *Offizierstellvertreter* (Officer Substitute) to suitable candidates. Again, it was hard to conceal the fact that the powers that be had made a disastrous mistake in not deciding to produce tanks of their own when the British and French armies were equipped with ever-increasing numbers. There could be no escaping the fact that if the Allies so wished they had the means to mount a major offensive, while Germany did not; nor was it easy to forget that families at home were no longer able to satisfy their hunger because of the Royal Navy's almost impenetrable blockade.

The Allies were planning a major offensive on the Amiens sector of the front, partly because the German advance during March had come dangerously close to capturing the town, beyond which lay the Somme estuary. The loss of the estuary would have separated the British and French armies, with potentially disastrous consequences, thus giving the removal of the threat a high priority. It would also recover important stretches of railway lost during the same offensive. The major blow would be delivered by General Sir Henry Rawlinson's Fourth Army, the right of which would be covered by General Marie Debeney's French First Army.

The major blow would be struck south of the Somme by the Canadian Corps (Lieutenant General Sir Arthur Currie) on the right and the Australian Corps (General Sir John Monash) on the left, beside the river, and III Corps (Lieutenant General Sir R. H. K. Butler) north of the river to safeguard the left flank of the attack. The Tank Corps had assembled its entire strength of fighting vehicles, including 324 Mark V and Mark V Star heavy tanks and ninety-six Whippets, the last specifically designed to support cavalry operations. In addition, forty-two fighting tanks were retained in mechanical reserve, 120 supply tanks (mainly older machines) including sixty-six allocated to infantry formations, were available to bring forward rations, ammunition, fuel and consolidation stores, and twenty-two gun carriers based on cut-down tank hulls and intended to provide infantry with immediate artillery support in newly captured sectors. Tanks were allocated as follows: the 1st, 4th, 5th and 14th Battalions – the Canadian Corps; the 2nd, 8th, 13th and 15th Battalions – the Australian Corps; the 10th Battalion; the 3rd and 6th Battalions – the Cavalry Corps.

We are, however, primarily concerned with the sixteen Austin armoured cars issued to the Tank Corps' 17th Battalion to extend the Australian Corps' exploitation capacity. These were the same cars that would have travelled to Mesopotamia with Duncars' vehicles had they not been retained in the United Kingdom and transferred to the 17th Battalion, commanded by Lieutenant Colonel E. J. Carter, for which no tanks were available. Some of the crews may have been disappointed at not having the opportunity to serve in tanks, although their new vehicles did possess various points of interest. The two turrets were armed with the standard Hotchkiss guns rather than the ball-mounted Vickers machine guns that had been fitted to Austin armoured cars purchased by Russia. Likewise, double rear wheels were fitted to Austins in British service. Duplicate front and rear steering positions were fitted, although only the front wheels were actually steered. The tyres were Rubberine, as mentioned in an earlier chapter, with ingenious stowage for spare wheels in the base of the turrets. The crews' only complaint was related to a weakness in the back axle which did not stand up well to hard usage. By the beginning of August the 17th Battalion had been in France long enough to be acclimatised to the Western Front and had taken part in the June battles while temporarily attached to the French.

The coming battle would take its name from the nearby city of Amiens. Preparations for it were carried out in deep secrecy, one aspect being to keep the German air force at a distance from the assembly areas so that it was unable to gather any useful information as to what was going on. The tanks moved into their assembly areas at the lowest possible speed to deaden the distinctive sounds of engines and tracks, but to reinforce security British aircraft also flew over the relevant areas during the period that movements were taking place. Despite this, Germans manning their forward trenches sent back regular reports of tank movement after dark. No attention was paid to these by senior headquarters who believed that the troops were suffering from 'tank phobia' and inclined to cry 'wolf' too often to be taken seriously. In fact, once in their assembly areas, the tanks were carefully camouflaged, all traces of movement were concealed and activity was reduced to an absolute minimum. Simultaneously, the artillery, which would concentrate on counter-battery work at zero hour followed by a rolling barrage rather than a sustained preparatory bombardment, was fixing its target details by accurate surveys that were constantly brought up to date. To ease suspicions, the British artillery did not vary its normal day to day programmes.

Zero Hour was 04.20 on 8 August. Approximately twelve minutes earlier the tanks began moving forward from their assembly areas one thousand yards to the rear. A heavy ground mist was welcomed as it provided protection from the enemy's artillery but, when added to the difficulties of a night march, caused a certain amount of delay. The armoured cars were each being towed behind a tank that would haul them across the trench lines which, as the enemy had only been in occupation of this sector for a comparatively short period, had not been developed to the same extent as those encountered at Cambrai and, being neither so deep nor so wide, did not require the provision of fascines to get across. Nevertheless, as the car crews were unable to control events themselves at this stage, it is unlikely that they were looking forward to this part of the advance.

As for the enemy, their front was held by seven under-strength divisions of General von der Marwitz's German Second Army, plus four more divisions in reserve. The average strength of these formations was about 3,000 men, but the Army's staff considered that only two divisions were still fit for active service. At 04.20 a huge series of flashes lit the western horizon, followed seconds later by the thunder of the guns themselves. As those in the trenches hastily stood to, the air was filled by the sound of ripping cloth as the first shells plunged down to explode in and around the trenches. Then came the warning shouts the occupants had been dreading – 'Panzer alarm!' From the British lines came the growing rumble of hundreds of engines and the tortured squealing of metal tracks. The SOS rockets sped skywards, their bursting light illuminating the long line of distinctive shapes. Rifle and machine-gun fire broke out along the trenches. Sparks confirmed bullet strikes against the enemy's armour plate, but still the tanks came on, returning the fire with their guns and automatic weapons. As they crushed their way through the wire entanglement, a flimsy thing by the standards of earlier years, a few Germans ran out to fling useless stick grenades, others fled to the rear or raised their arms in surrender. Isolated groups, usually machine-gun teams, continued to fire at the enemy infantry following the tanks, only to be blown away horribly by a blast of 6-pounder canister fired by one of the tanks. This was one of the most fiendish types of ammunition ever devised, consisting of numerous small metal balls joined together by wire; the fearful results this produced as it coned out on leaving the gun's muzzle can well be imagined.

During this part of the action the armoured car crews were flung about and received injuries of varying severity unless they took note of the driver's shouted instructions. In the misty darkness the driver alone of the crew could predict the probable course his vehicle would take by carefully watching the movements of the towing tank through his vision slit and giving warnings of sudden drops, inclines and sideways slopes. Once clear of the trench system and in better light men from both crews would dismount to disconnect the towing chain, after which the vehicle would continue with the tasks as previously ordered. This was not always easy as the mist hung heavily, involving some confusion as vehicles sought the correct route forward. Once this had been sorted out the armoured cars wrote one of the most remarkable pages in the entire history of the Royal Armoured Corps.

It was almost midnight when Colonel Carter, red-eyed from lack of sleep, grubby from head to foot and stained with oil and grease, returned to the Headquarters of the Australian Corps to make his report to General Sir John Monash. The General listened and then ordered one of his clerks to take down Carter's story, almost verbatim. In 1959 what he said was recorded in the first volume of the Royal Tank Regiment's history, *The Tanks*, by Basil Liddell Hart:

Got armoured cars through to Warfusee-Abancourt. When we reached the other side of no man's land we found that the road was good but a number of trees (large and small) had been shot down and lay right across it in places. Obstacles removed by chopping up the smaller trees and hauling off the big ones by means of a tank. Pioneers helped us to clear the road all the way down. We did not come up to our advancing troops until they were almost near the Red Line (one of several bounds/report lines designated by colour). When we got past our leading infantry we came upon quite a number of Huns and dealt with them. Had then to wait a little on account of our barrage, but went through a light barrage. When we got to Blue Line we detached three sections to run down to Framerville. When they got there they found all the Boche horse transport and many lorries drawn up in the main road ready to move off. Head of column tried to bolt in one direction and other vehicles in another. Complete confusion. Our men killed the lot using 3,000 rounds and left them there; four Staff Officers on horseback shot also. The cars then ran down to the east side of Harbonnieres, on the south-east road to Vauvillers and met there a number of steam wagons; fired into their boilers causing an impossible block. Had a lot of good shooting around Vauvillers. Then came back to main road. Two sections of cars went on to Foucaucourt and came in contact with a Boche gun in a wood north-east of Foucaucourt. This gun blew the wheels off one car and also hit three others. However, three of the cars got away. Two other cars went to Proyart and found a lot of troops billeted there having lunch in the houses. Our cars shot through the windows into the houses, killing quite a lot of the enemy. Another section went towards Chuignolles and found it full of German soldiers. Our cars shot them. Found rest billets and old trenches also with troops in them. Engaged them. Had quite a battle there. Extent of damage not known, but considerable. Cars then came back to main road. We were then well in advance of Blue Line. Everything was now perfectly quiet – no shellfire of any kind.

I went a quarter of a mile beyond La Flaque. There was a big dump there, and the Huns kept continually coming out and surrendering, and we brought quite a lot of them back as prisoners. It was then about 10.30. A party of Huns was detailed to tow back a disabled car. I saw no sign of any (barbed) wire system anywhere. Old overgrown trenches but no organised trench system. I proceeded to some rising ground near Framerville. Did not go into Framerville, but could see that the roofs of the houses were intact. Saw no trace of any organised system of defence of any kind and no troops. My people saw no formed bodies of troops of any kind during the day coming towards us, but very large numbers of fugitives hastening in the opposite direction. Engaged as many of them as could be reached from the roads. I saw, from the hill, open country with a certain amount of vegetation on it.

It might seem a little strange that Carter does not mention that the regiment's two leading cars, commanded by Lieutenant E. J. Rollings, had entered Framerville and shot up a German advanced corps headquarters there. Among the files they captured was the defence scheme, complete in every detail, of the twenty-mile stretch of the Hindenburg Line between the Oise and Bellicourt, information that proved to be priceless when plans were being drawn up for the British attack on these defences. It seems probable that Rollings handed over his discovery to senior officers at the first opportunity and did not meet Carter again until the following morning. Carter's notes were dictated by a tired man at the end of an exhausting day and he would certainly have included some mention of Rollings' astonishing *coup* had he been aware of it.

If one under-strength armoured car regiment could achieve results like this, one might expect the achievements of two regiments of Whippet medium tanks to exceed them by a very wide margin. It was most unfortunate that the Whippets were placed under the command of the cavalry when a previous exercise or two would have demonstrated that the two were completely incompatible. On the day itself the cavalry cantered ahead until opposition in the form of machine guns was encountered, and then found some suitable dead ground in which to shelter until the slower Whippets arrived and dealt with the problem. Then the cavalry would be off again until it encountered more opposition and had to wait until the Whippets arrived. However, one tank commander, Lieutenant Clement Arnold, quickly tired of this silly game and set off with his Whippet, named *Musical Box*, into the enemy's rear areas where he continued to cause absolute mayhem until 15.00 when a shell from a German field gun ignited the results of a petrol leak, forcing the crew to abandon the vehicle. They all sustained burns and would have been killed on the spot had it not been for the intervention of a German officer. Several days later the advance caught up with *Musical Box*, now gutted and alone, over seven miles behind the original German front line. Only when Arnold was released from prison camp at the end of the war did the details of his incredible foray become known.

The Battle of Amiens lasted from 8 to 11 August. On the first day the British penetrated to a depth of seven and a half miles but thereafter progress was slower. On 8 August, 12,415 Germans were taken prisoner, including 281 officers. Ludendorff, in overall command of the German Army, described the date as 'the Black Day of the German Army' and advised the Kaiser that victory was no longer possible. He was particularly unsettled by the percentage of officers who had chosen to surrender, indicating a growth of the view that there was no longer any point in continuing to fight. By the end of the battle the Germans had sustained over 75,000 casualties. The battle initiated the slow but sustained Allied advance which continued for the remainder of the war.

Having taken part in this, the armoured cars of the Tank Corps' 17th Battalion enjoyed one more claim to fame in the days following the Armistice. Flying the identical brown, red and green flag flown by Brigadier Hugh Elles as he led his tanks into battle at Cambrai, the battalion had the privilege of leading the British Army of Occupation over the Rhine and into Cologne.

Bibliography

Anglesey, the Marquess of, *A History of the British Cavalry Vol. 5 1914–1917, Egypt, Palestine and Syria* (Leo Cooper, Barnsley, 1994)

Barker, A. J., *Townshend of Kut* (Cassell & Co., London, 1967)

Carver, Field Marshal Lord, *The Turkish Front 1914–18, Gallipoli, Mesopotamia and Palestine* (Pan, London, 2004)

Dunsterville, Major General L.C., *The Adventures of Dunsterforce* (Edward Arnold, London, 1920)

Falls, Cyril, *Armageddon 1918* (Weidenfeld & Nicolson, London, 1964)

Fletcher, David, *War Cars – British Armoured Cars in the First World War*, (HMSO, London, 1987)

Forty, George, *The Royal Tank Regiment – A Pictorial History* (Guild, Tunbridge Wells, 1989)

Kutz, C. R., *War on Wheels – The Evolution of an Idea* (The Scientific Book Club, London, 1942)

Liddell Hart, Basil, *The Tanks – The History of the Royal Tank Regiment 1914–1939* (Cassell & Co., London, 1959)

Mosley, Leonard, *Duel for Kilimanjaro – The East African Campaign 1914–1918* (Weidenfeld & Nicolson, London, 1963)

Perrett, Bryan and Lord, Anthony, *The Czar's British Squadron* (William Kimber, London, 1981)

Perrett, Bryan, *Iron Fist – Classic Armoured Warfare Case Studies* (Arms & Armour Press, London, 1995)

——, *Desert Warfare – From Its Roman Origins to the Gulf Conflict* (Patrick Stevens Ltd, Wellingborough, 1988)

Purnell, *History of the First World War*, Vols 1–8 (London)

White, B. T., *Tanks and Other Fighting Vehicles 1914-1918* (Blandford, London, 1970)

——, *British Tanks and Fighting Vehicles 1914–1945* (Ian Allan, London, 1970)

Index